Running With The Bulls

David Kitching

Cover Illustration: Prehistoric Auroch, the ancestor of modern bulls

From an original oil painting by David Kitching

Copyright © 2017 David Kitching

All rights reserved.

ISBN: 9781549553479

DEDICATION

To Saint Christopher, patron saint of travellers.

CONTENTS

1: Prologue – High Plains Drifting
2: One Year Earlier – Lytham Cemetery, Lancashire
3: Intrigue and Preparation
4: October – Heading South
5: November – Falkland Islands Impressions
6: November – Kayaking in South Georgia
7: December – Yucatan Peninsula, Mexico
8: December – La Vuelta a Puerto Escondido
9: January – A Journey Through Mesoamerica
10: February – All Aboard El Chepe to the Copper Canyon
11: February – Whales and Sharks in the Sea of Cortez
12: March – In search of the Giraffe Necked Weevil
13: April – On tour in the Western Cape
14: May – Camping on the Roof of Africa
15: June – Sri Lankan Diaries
16: July – Trekking in Nepal
17: August – Sailing in Thailand
18: August – Cycling in Chiang Mai
19: August – Indonesian Volcanoes and Dragons
20: September – Rugby World Cup in New Zealand
21: October – The Tournament Reaches its Climax
22: November – Sailing in Tonga
23: November – Polynesian Paradise
24: December – Easter Island's Moai Mystery
25: Epilogue – Returning Home

ACKNOWLEDGEMENTS

I would like to thank all those people who read my numerous travel updates over the years and whose kind words encouraged me to believe that one day I might be able to write this book.

CHAPTER 1
PROLOGUE - HIGH PLAINS DRIFTING

With the early morning sun glinting off its fuselage, the tiny fifteen seater Dornier appeared as a mere speck on the towering Himalayan rock formation which opposed it. The feisty little plane seemed to be flexing every fibre of its being and, with the Nepali pilot giving it full throttle, it only just cleared the top of the highest pass between Pokhara and Jomsom. It instantly banked sharply to the right, sweeping down over dark wooded slopes and glistening glaciers en route to Jomsom airport. The pilot seemed to hit the runway hard, braking noisily to stop the Dornier running on in the thin air. This was all in a day's work for the pilot. Not so for us. We could scarcely have had a more exciting ride had we purchased a ticket for the Big One at Blackpool Pleasure Beach.

This was the opening scene of our trekking trip to Nepal's Upper Mustang restricted area. Upper Mustang is a remote part of Northern Nepal surrounded on three sides by Tibet. In order to preserve local culture and restrict access to foreigners, a guide is compulsory and, at five hundred US dollars per person, the permit itself is much more expensive than for other treks. Recently a controversial new road has opened connecting it to the rest of Nepal.

It's an area we've always wanted to visit and the Nepalese economy is constantly in need of support. As independent trekking is not an option in Upper Mustang, we asked Chandra, our trekking agent from 'Himalaya Guide Nepal' in Kathmandu, to put together in effect our own miniature Himalayan expedition. In addition to the compulsory guide, we also requested a porter. Chandra organised all flights, transport and accommodation. Before leaving Kathmandu we learnt we would be joined at late notice by Ai Lei, a young Taiwanese lady we had never met, and her porter.

High on the Tibetan Plateau, Upper Mustang is the realm of the Snow Leopard. Its Tibetan Buddhist culture is unique and it is possibly a window on what Tibet was like before the 1950s Chinese invasion. Here one woman can have two husbands. My wife Jan was particularly keen to embrace this new culture!

Geographically, the area is very dry due to a localised

rain shadow effect. Hot and sunny during the day and freezing cold at night, it is in effect a high altitude desert. Its stark scenery is very unlike any other trek in Nepal. Think perhaps of Arizona's Grand Canyon or Mexico's Copper Canyon.

The amazing walk takes you north following the broad stony river bars of the Kali Kandaki towards the river's source high up on the Tibetan Plateau. Soon the trail gains elevation as the enormous canyons start to tower above the river, sculpted and eroded by the ever present dry wind blowing up from the south. To the south the snow capped giants of the Annapurna range look on with obvious approval. It is truly a place beyond the wit of mortal poets.

A trek in Nepal is always challenging. Wonderful during the day due to the monumental scenery, at night the experience is quite ascetic. Though the food is wholesome the lodges are very basic, noisy and cold. Lights, door locks and many other things often don't work. The showers, if they exist, are always cold. The toilet is a mere hole in the ground. You've got to really love the mountains to come trekking in Nepal!

We all started the trek well, quickly acclimatising to the altitude. I have never felt better and was particularly strong ascending. Jan was steady paced and soon showing all her trademark dogged resilience, preferring ascending to her rather nervous descending. Ai Lei, as well as lowering the team's average age considerably, fitted in well and seemed very fit. For our Nepali guide and porters, all around twenty and born at altitude, it would be a stroll in the park. On paper we looked easily capable of getting up to Lo Mantang, capital of Upper Mustang, at around 3,800 metres in six days. No way would the enterprise fail on my account.

How wrong can you be? Within a couple of days I caught a nasty cold. After spending a long and horrible night at Charang (around 3,500 metres) gasping for air, it seemed reckless to ascend any further. Over breakfast next morning plans were hastily made for an orderly retreat. The group would split up temporarily and we would retrace our steps towards the safety of lower altitudes. It was a good call and I soon recovered.

Though we never quite made it to the fabled city of Lo Mantang it was still a hugely enjoyable trek. The return journey from the top of the Tibetan Plateau was visually stunning with the added cultural dimension of our visits to Tibetan Buddhist monasteries so atmospheric that they transport you back through time itself.

Our only reservation was the road. Perhaps eighty percent of the trek is on the road and, though it is not busy, it is annoying to have to step off the trail to let jeeps and bikes go by, only to have dust blown in your face for your troubles. I suspect longer term the number of trekkers will diminish with the slack being taken up by local tourists. The locals we spoke to seemed to like the road for economic reasons but I suspect their culture will be affected just as surely as if the Chinese had invaded. As long as locals made the decision and not some bureaucrat in Kathmandu I don't really have a problem with that.

We've decided to take a leaf out of the UK banking industry's books with their "Rewards for failure" philosophy. Following our failed expedition we've awarded ourselves a special bonus in the form of a few days in a comfortable beach hotel in Phuket, Thailand. I'm sure it will be very pleasant if a little mainstream and boring. But perhaps that's what we need now after the discomforts of trekking in Nepal!

CHAPTER 2
ONE YEAR EARLIER LYTHAM CEMETERY, LANCASHIRE

The day of the funeral dawned cold and damp. This was after all Lancashire. A stiff cutting breeze blew in off the Irish Sea, the barometer was falling away and grey skies hung ominously over the Fylde coast. This was the place where I'd been brought up. Though it was normally an enjoyable experience to revisit my roots and those places holding so many youthful memories, this day was anything but pleasant. Like the weather my mood was gloomy and somber.

The body in the casket had in life belonged to my oldest friend, Graham. Having met on day one of our first year at grammar school, we'd really grown up together, negotiating more or less successfully all those bitter sweet rites of passage that accompany that perilous transition from boyhood to manhood. We even studied the same subjects at O and A level, eventually finishing up reading the same subject at university. At that point our paths diverged, he choosing the legal profession and myself, determined not to be outdone in the excitement stakes, ending up as an accountant. Not before I'd been best man at his wedding though.

The circumstances of his unfortunate death were bizarre in the extreme. He had always spoken with passion of his burning desire to run with the bulls in Pamplona. That much I'd known for ages. The rest I was only now at the funeral learning about from his family. Once he'd reached financial security at age fifty, he promptly retired, withdrawing a chunk of equity from the Liverpool based firm of solicitors of which he had been Senior Partner. Within weeks he had booked his flight to Spain. Though his wife had misgivings, she loved him and so reluctantly granted him leave of absence, knowing how much the bulls meant to him. He was fighting fit and ready to go.

But, to paraphrase a famous Scottish poet, the best laid plans of mice and men often come to very little. Having reviewed his bovine adversaries on the day of the race, he decided to warm up on the narrow cobbled streets by doing a few sprint repetitions. Tragically he accidentally put his foot in a cowpat, falling over backwards and hitting his head on the curbstone. He was immediately unconscious, soon falling into a coma from which he never recovered.

Sadly, within a couple of hours he had bid adios to this mortal struggle. At least he never suffered. He had come so close to fulfilling his Pamplona dreams, but not close enough. He had died too early with unfinished business in life. Not to mention the unpaid bar bill at his hotel.

Back by the graveside, as I fought back the tears, I thought also of my own mortality, my own life and death. How many of my own dreams would never come to fruition, how many items on my bucket list would never actually be realised during my allotted lifespan? I could not know the time of my own passing nor its manner. Would it be early or later? That I would never know, nor in reality would I wish to. What I could however control were my own actions prior to that. By ensuring that I wasted no time in executing my bucket list and completing its contents sooner rather than later, I would not only have a great time but, by banking these experiences at the earliest available opportunity, death itself, when the Reaper eventually called me, would be much less of a problem. Now was the time to seize the day. It would be misleading to suggest that these thoughts had only just come about at this point in time. In reality they had been rattling around within my subconscious for some time now. What the funeral did was to bring them into much sharper focus. I would now seize the day. By the time the humanist eulogy had been delivered, these words, hitherto vague, sketchy and ethereal, were now etched indelibly on my consciousness with all of the subtlety and understatement of Blackpool's seasonal Illuminations just a few miles up the coast. Seize the day... seize the day... I would run with my own metaphorical bulls before it was too late... With a bit of luck I would also avoid the bullshit...

Pamplona had certainly never been on my bucket list but lots of other places were. I wanted to kayak with penguins in Antarctica, spend weeks touring Mexico's archaeological sites, trek in the high Himalaya, sail in Tonga and a whole lot more. You can of course do these things during your annual vacation as long as you don't mind feeling shattered from the stresses of work in your first week and dreading your return during your second. This time it would be different. We would give ourselves the time and space to really appreciate things. We'd travelled widely in the past but this would be something else, something wonderful.

Then, inexplicably, back at the funeral something sinister happened. The dark clad mourners gathered by the graveside turned one by one to face me. They pointed to a second casket. It was open and empty. Engraved on the nameplate I read out with horror my own name. The mourners silently moved towards me, firmly ushering me in its direction. I realised what was happening but far too late and tried to run. My legs were rooted to the spot. I kicked out in desperation. Then there was only darkness.

I awoke with a start in my bedroom in Surrey. My long suffering wife Jan was clutching her right calf muscle whilst complaining vociferously that I'd kicked her, and why was I such a great oaf? It had all been a bad dream. It was four o'clock in the morning. Apologising profusely to her for my inadvertent act of domestic violence, I sighed heavily with relief, heading off to make a cup of tea in the land of the living.

Both Graham and I were still alive. It was all just a dream, a silly nightmare. It meant nothing, I told myself.

Several hours later I wasn't so sure though. We are of course the architects of our own dreams. We write the scripts. Dreams are a window into our subconscious, that inner repository of our most basic fears and insecurities. Those unresolved uncertainties that silently stalk us in the dead of night when we are at our most vulnerable.

As for my dream, you didn't need to be a genius to work this one out. Graham and I were indeed both in rude good health and would live to fight another day. But in addition to the physical body there is a thing called the human soul. The spirit that dares to dream and which needs constant nourishment over and above the grind of daily routine. The fact still remained that he had never been to Pamplona and I had never really travelled, not in the way I had always wanted to. I could not of course answer for him. But for me it was high time to put things right, sooner rather than later. Before I had any further nightmares.

CHAPTER 3
INTRIGUE AND PREPARATION

By an extraordinary stroke of fate shortly after my Martin Luther King moment (though in my case it was more a nightmare than a dream), Jan discovered that she was about to lose her job and that her employer would hand over a large sum of money in compensation. The corporate restructuring had been going on for some time but the announcement was still a shock. What might have earlier been considered a setback was now looking more and more like an opportunity. My own temporary contract was coming to an end so the timing was perfect. In my own career I couldn't help thinking that I'd seen one balance sheet too many and a change was needed. There is a tide in the affairs of men...

However, first I needed to persuade Jan. I suspected it wouldn't be too difficult as she loves travelling. If ordinary diplomacy proved fruitless I had at the back of my mind a cunning and devious plan. Jan is a big rugby fan. If we could somehow tailor our trip to take in the 2011 Rugby World Cup in New Zealand she would definitely fall under my spell. Armed with this Machiavellian strategy, I carefully broached the subject. I needn't have worried though. She was ahead of the game. "What took you so long?" was her reply. All systems were go!

We began to plan the trip. For this we needed to know what we could and couldn't do depending on the season prevailing in our chosen countries. For example, it would be difficult or impossible to trek in certain countries in the rainy season and certain wildlife encounters would only be possible at very specific times of year. Antarctica would only present a brief window of opportunity in the Southern Hemisphere's summer. The order in which we visited countries was therefore key, but we also wanted a sensible routing to keep travel costs down and with it our carbon footprint.

There was much to consider. Would we buy "Round the world tickets" which are potentially cheaper if you are travelling continuously either west or east? Would their complexity and restrictions mean us going for individual discounted tickets instead to afford greater flexibility? We would certainly need backpacker insurance. A pre-loaded currency card would be a convenient way to give us access to ATMs given that banks and credit card companies are forever cancelling your cards, even if you tell them exactly where you're going abroad. We'd need a secret emergency stash of US dollars sewn into our rucksacks. Which countries would require visas to be purchased in the UK and which would much more conveniently issue them to us on arrival? Who would look after our house? Who would tend our large garden in our absence during our year away? There were a million and one things to organise but it would all be worth it.

What would our travelling style be? Everyone likes to think of himself as a traveller not a tourist. We would spend a bare minimum of time in big cities. Just enough time to make our travelling arrangements. Big cities are all very similar these days in such a globalised, linked and multi cultural world. With the exception of a few highlights, we would get out into the smaller towns, the countryside and the places where our chosen activities were based. That way we would hopefully get a better insight into the distinct culture of our chosen country, the character of its people, and hopefully reach out to its heart and soul. We would not stick slavishly to all the "Must do" highlights of the big tour companies. If a so called big highlight didn't interest us we simply wouldn't do it.

Instead we would seek to slow things down and savour the moment. We would try to get off the tourist circuit and visit those smaller less frequented places where the unique character of a country would hopefully reveal itself. You don't travel to see things that are the same as your own culture. The attraction is to experience and see other cultures and ways of living that are distinct and different and therefore interesting.

We would travel independently but if we needed a tour we would choose a local tour operator. This would be cheaper for us and good for local jobs. We would certainly brush up our rusty Spanish for South America rather than relying on others speaking English. This would enable us to travel off the beaten track. On seeing a look of incomprehension we would never just repeat our English in a louder voice! We would be open and friendly but hopefully not naive. We would try to travel with a smile on our faces, which given what we were proposing shouldn't be too difficult. The difficult part might be still smiling when we came home!

With a couple of exceptions, apart from the flights, insurance and the first few nights' accommodation, remarkably little else had been booked. With our iPad Mini we would be able to book things as we went as internet cafes are not always so common these days, depending on where you are in the world.

As the day of departure loomed it was hard to believe that we were leaving a comfortable rural existence in our sleepy Surrey village and taking a step into the unknown. On the afternoon of the flight I glanced rather wistfully and nervously out of the taxi window at the autumnal hues of the Surrey Hills, trying to take in the enormity of what we had set out to do. In just over one year's time when we return, autumn will already have surrendered to the hardships of winter. Our taxi soon sped around the smooth tarmac of the M25 on route to Heathrow. First stop South America. TAM would take us to Sao Paolo and then LAN Chile onwards to Buenos Aires. Then it would all begin. Would we live to regret it or would it be the making of us? There was only one way to find out. I could almost taste that first glass of Malbec...

That's all in the past now. Going forward, we'll keep you posted with frequent travelogues, which Jan and I will compose along the way, as we experience the thrills and spills of our marathon trip. Our plan is to live in the present and simply enjoy the moment, free of the past and unconcerned about the future.

CHAPTER 4
OCTOBER - HEADING SOUTH

We are currently staying in the remote Patagonian city of Ushuaia, the world's most southerly town, about to embark on what, even to seasoned travellers like ourselves, is the trip of a lifetime. Tomorrow we board the Ocean Diamond, a purpose built Antarctic expedition ship, and set sail on a three week voyage to the Falkland Islands, South Georgia and Antarctica. On board will be the two kayaks we have ordered with which we are hoping to get face to face with penguins and seals amongst the ice flows.

We've actually spent the last ten days in Patagonia in order to break up the long journey south but also to enjoy the warm sunny weather of the South American spring, before heading down to the frozen continent that will forever be associated with Shackleton and Scott.

After a couple of days resting in Buenos Aires following our long haul flight from Heathrow (surely the modern equivalent of being subjected to the Spanish Inquisition), we promptly headed down to a place we've always wanted to see. It is the World Heritage site of Peninsula Valdez on the Patagonian coast. It was here that David Attenborough shot his sensational footage of orcas intentionally beaching themselves to hunt sea lion pups. We hired a car for a week from nearby Puerto Madryn and clocked over fifteen hundred kilometres on the dusty gravel roads of Patagonia. We also took in Cabo Dos Bahias, remote and three hundred kilometres further to the south, where there is a penguin colony or pinguineria.

Though we didn't actually see orcas beaching themselves whilst hunting, we did see some orcas and a host of other wildlife, much of it unique to South America such as guanacos and rheas. On the very first day, as I was swimming and Jan paddling, she enthusiastically attracted my attention to announce that something wonderful had just happened. She went on to explain that an inquisitive penguin, travelling at the speed of a torpedo, had just buzzed her at extremely close range in the shallows. Then, the following day a practically tame armadillo tried to join us for lunch. But this was just a foretaste of what this peninsula can offer the visitor.

Peninsula Valdez is famous for its Southern Right

Whales who come here to mate and calve at this time of year. It is a great privilege to get close to such magnificent creatures and their calves. Often they are so close to the shore that you don't need a boat to go whale watching. The sight of a fifty ton animal leaving the water and breaching nearby is something you never really forget. Or a whale raising its barnacle encrusted head to look you in the eye. Or perhaps a mother tending her calf just a few metres off the beach. It is a truly amazing place.

At Cabos Dos Bahias we practically had the pinguineria to ourselves, making it a very exclusive wildlife viewing experience. I have to admit that we returned a couple of times to linger with these tough little Jackass Penguins, who seem to take the challenges of life in the tempestuous South Atlantic totally in their stride. Their name derives from the fact they make donkey like braying sounds.

Before dropping off the hire car in Puerto Madryn we paid a visit to Trelew. This part of Patagonia is known as Welsh Patagonia. The Welsh arrived in 1865. They had migrated from their native Wales to protect Welsh language and culture which they considered to be under grave threat from the global march of the English language. Whilst strolling along the beach front in Puerto Madryn, we came across a memorial plaque marking the actual place where these hardy pioneers had come ashore before moving inland.

Now, one hundred and fifty years on, such is the pride in their origins and culture that a dialect of Welsh is still spoken here today. Though their dialects are different, modern Welshmen and Patagonians can still communicate. Rather than being divided by a common language, they are unified by an uncommon one. In Trelew even some Argentinians of non Welsh descent learn a little Welsh at night school for reasons of social prestige.

However, our main purpose in coming to Trelew was to see the impressive Museum of Palaeontology. Patagonia is famous for the sheer number of fossilized dinosaur remains found here. Many of them seem to be housed in this museum. It has an incredible number of intact dinosaur skeletons beautifully displayed and described. Not surprisingly, most of the explanations are in Spanish, with some English translations. This was good for our Spanish. They also play a BBC film with Spanish subtitles which is fascinating.

The film explains the eventual demise of Patagonia's dinosaurs. It was nothing to do with a lack of adaptability but down to the chain of events unleashed by a meteorite collision sixty five million years ago. It is unlikely modern man would survive such a catastrophe. If the meteorite had missed the earth or landed in deeper water it's likely the dinosaurs would still be around today and we wouldn't. You just don't know what is around the corner in life. We paused for a moment to consider the fate of the creatures whose bones were displayed in front of us. Suitably chastened and not knowing what the future might bring, we left the excellent museum even more determined to seize the day and enjoy the rest of our trip.

From Chubut we flew to El Calafate. Patagonia really is an enormous place that encompasses much of southern Argentina and Chile. Having seen the impressive Perito Moreno glacier and toasted it with a glass of Argentine whisky and glacier ice, we headed to El Chalten to do some trekking in the Fitzroy range of Los Glaciares National Park. Named after the captain of Darwin's ship the "Beagle", Fitzroy is the Argentine equivalent of Chile's Torres Del Paine National Park. The two ranges share the same geology. We spent several days doing day hikes, marvelling at the trademark craggy peaks. The highest peak here is only 3,400 metres, small compared to the Andes further north around Mendoza, but the southerly latitude means it can get cold even during the summer. So, rather than camp, we hiked by day and enjoyed the comforts of a warm lodge and a glass of Andes or Quilmes in the evening. On one hike we saw a solitary condor elegantly and effortlessly riding the thermals whilst it checked us out. We thought it best to keep moving!

We really like Argentina and could quite happily live here. The people are friendly and there is plenty of living space. It is in effect a European country in South America, certainly more prosperous than some of its neighbours such as Bolivia. I think a lady we spoke to at a bus station summed it up rather well when she said it was a country of great potential but "Muy mal administrado". A hundred years ago it was one of the richest countries in the world but it has never really realised its potential more recently.

So it is no surprise that the Argentine economy is in its usual precarious state. Nobody trusts the peso and everyone wants to hold a relatively stable currency like the US dollar. The official exchange rate is one figure but on the black market it is about fifty percent higher. However tempting, it is bit risky changing your dollars with currency touts on the street. What you need is a friendly hotel owner keen to have a hedge against future rampant inflation and devaluations. Once you have your pesos at this improved rate, the country is not nearly so expensive.

Having had our sunshine and rest, it is time to face the penguins in a kayak. I hope to have something more substantial to tell you in three weeks' time, unless of course I have been eaten by a Leopard Seal!

CHAPTER 5
NOVEMBER - FALKLAND ISLANDS IMPRESSIONS

After what seemed like an eternity of anticipation, the Ocean Diamond finally threw off her lines in the Argentine port of Ushuaia and headed purposefully out into the Beagle Channel, sailing east and following the coast of South America towards the Falkland Islands.

This initial feeling of excitement and euphoria would not last long however, as within a few hours the two hundred passenger ship was rolling from side to side in the storm that had been forecast before departure. The Captain had tried to linger in the Beagle Channel for as long as possible to give the storm a chance to blow itself out but this strategy was only partially successful. As we pitifully languished in our cabin feeling sorry for ourselves, this was just a taste of what the sea can do in this part of the world and we weren't even yet in the Drake Passage, where the coast of South America runs out and there is no land at all to break up the swell. It was better really to be on deck with gaze fixed on the horizon or watching the Giant Petrels and Wandering Albatrosses skimming the waves in what were easy conditions for them. I'm not sure if seeing them so much at home made me feel better or worse.

The following day, as the storm blew itself out and we started to get our sea legs, it was time to get used to life on board. Never having cruised before, I had always thought of cruises as providing activities like bingo and entertainments that might be a mixture of "Blind Date" and "Strictly Come Dancing". However this cruise was infinitely more cerebral. Apart from the mandatory briefings on forthcoming activities and landings, there were optional lectures on geology, polar history, marine biology, ornithology, photography and many other related subjects.

Our first stop was the Falkland Islands. After spending the previous day visiting wonderful penguin and albatross colonies on Carcass Island and Saunders Island, we arrived at Port Stanley, the capital, just before breakfast. Seen from the inner harbour, Stanley is a colourful collection of houses and buildings extending up the hillside. Just over the brow of the hill is the Stanley Bypass (the M25 of Stanley), which is entirely devoid of traffic. In fact, there are only two and a half thousand people in the whole of the Falklands and all the cars are either Land Rovers or Range Rovers, available for sale in a local dealership. Practically all have stickers proclaiming the drivers' allegiance to Britain.

It looks a pretty affluent place. Sheep farming has given way to fishing and tourism, with future oil revenues a possibility. It is now much more open than it was prior to the 1982 war, with more of a healthy influx of other nationalities. There is very much a feeling that if you want a job you can get one. I think it is probably much more economically viable than prior to the war, though the subsidy from the UK taxpayer must still be enormous.

It is an interesting place. Once ferried ashore we immediately headed into a small gift shop on the very British promenade. The shop was completely empty and, though we made a few token purchases, we really wanted to chat with a Falkland Islander. The proprietor was about our age (early fifties) and had only left the islands twice, both times to England. She had lived through the Argentine invasion and during her trip to England had found London overwhelming and unfriendly, which of course it is. Our long chat was a fascinating insight on many levels and having these sorts of conversations is really one of the reasons why you travel.

In such a quiet and isolated place inevitably the 1982

conflict still casts a long shadow. On the main promenade there is a moving memorial to the Falklands War listing all the UK nationals who died by name. Nearby is "Thatcher Drive". Because of the news footage from the 1980's you almost feel you already know this place. Nothing prepares you for the feeling of isolation though.

We have a very interesting Cambridge educated polar historian on board. Looking back to the outbreak of war, it is shocking just how many warning signs and vital pieces of intelligence regarding Argentine intentions were ignored by the British Government. It would have made a great script for one of the more farcical episodes of "Yes Prime Minister" had it not had such tragic consequences. But both General Galtieri and Prime Minister Thatcher were deeply unpopular at home and it could be argued that both needed a distraction from domestic affairs to boost their popularity. I hope however this analysis is incorrect – I much prefer good old fashioned honest but incompetent politicians to devious ones!

However, there are a few positive effects of the bitter war. The Falklands in 1982 was quite backward (by their own admission) but it is now a much more confident, outward facing and positive place. Argentina lost its military dictatorship and is now much more democratic. The UK got four more years of Margaret Thatcher. Who was it that won the war?

Only joking!

Having said goodbye to our friend in the gift shop, we spent the rest of the morning wandering around Stanley. We stood in silence for a while at the impressive Memorial, peered into the garden at Government House, visited a couple of museums and went for a typically British cup of tea. In fact the Falklands Islands are a little piece of Britain in the wilderness of the South Atlantic. We were even able to use some leftover sterling to pay for our cup of tea. I'm really glad we made the trip but it was perhaps all a little too familiar to really fascinate us.

David Kitching

CHAPTER 6
NOVEMBER - KAYAKING IN SOUTH GEORGIA AND ANTARCTICA

Two days after heading east from the Falklands we arrived at the sub Antarctic island of South Georgia, one of the most isolated places on earth. It is as though someone took the Alps and placed them in the middle of the South Atlantic. Rugged snow clad mountains up to 3,000 metres high and giant glaciers plummet dramatically to the surrounding freezing krill rich seas.

In terms of wildlife, South Georgia is the Galapagos Islands of the sub Antarctic. There are enormous colonies of many different species of penguins, sea birds and seals. Though there are whales (we saw Humpback, Fin, Orca, and Minke), they are not so numerous as they have been much slower to recover from hunting than the Fur Seals, despite shore based whaling finally ceasing here in the 1960s. This was not for any moral reasons but simply because the whalers had driven whales to the brink of extinction locally and therefore no longer had a land based industry. This minor detail would not stop them carrying on the persecution using factory ships till the 1980s.

These days the environment of South Georgia is closely regulated by the UK Government. Fishing licences are tightly controlled based on principles of sustainability. There are eradication programmes for such introduced species as reindeer, rats and mice to protect native bird populations. Before you go ashore you need to clean your boots and have your outer clothing vacuum cleaned. You even have to sign a "Biosecurity declaration" form promising not to introduce any seeds or soil onto the island. A little over the top possibly but a big improvement on the old days when you could just pitch up and club a Fur Seal to death or harpoon a whale.

The kayaking in South Georgia is fantastic. Kayaking is a silent, intimate way to explore the marine environment and gives you a real sense of freedom when compared to the numerous rules and regulations which trips ashore or boat excursions seem to entail. The water here is cold so you need many layers of clothing under the full dry suit that is necessary just in case you turn the kayak over. We had absolutely no intention of doing this! It is wonderful to be out on the water only a few metres away from a massive bull Elephant Seal or have half a dozen porpoising penguins cut across your bows. We even had a Fur Seal jump out of the water and almost land in the front of the kayak! In general the Elephant Seals have a more placid nature than the smaller Fur Seals.

We visited the old whaling station at Grytviken, from where Ernest Shackleton had launched his ill fated Endurance expedition at the end of that classical period of Edwardian polar exploration. The old whaling station has now been restored and they have built a small museum at a total cost of six and a half million pounds. We managed to visit the small cemetery where Shackleton was finally laid to rest in 1922 in a simple whalers' grave overlooking the sea, for so long on my bucket list. On the way to the graveyard you have to be careful not to disturb the King Penguins, Elephant Seals and Fur Seals which stubbornly block your way and clearly regard the place as their own.

However, there is still much to do in terms of conservation work on South Georgia. The other old, rusting and decaying whaling stations are a real eyesore and a potential hazard to wildlife. Having destroyed whale populations and made vast amounts of money, the whaling companies simply pulled out without doing a proper environmental clean up, leaving others to pick up the bill.

On route to the Antarctic Peninsula we also passed Elephant Island, the place where most of Shackleton's men spent four months awaiting his uncertain return, following his epic voyage of survival in a small boat to South Georgia. Elephant Island is an indescribably desolate and windswept place. It was being battered by freezing winds gusting up to fifty miles per hour as we passed by and I cannot imagine spending four hours there, let alone four months. After a few minutes out on deck I had to go back inside to warm up.

The Antarctic Peninsula itself is much more sheltered and we were able to do six very special sea kayaking excursions. On some trips, despite all the clothing, you would be paddling into a snow blizzard with your face numb with cold and feet feeling like blocks of ice, wondering what on earth had possessed you to sign up for such madness. A few hours later the sun would be out and the sea like a mill pond, enabling you to paddle amongst the exquisitely sculpted blue icebergs or with seals and penguins, navigating a precarious path through the strange forms and confusion of the pack ice. Then, this impossibly beautiful silent continent would seem like the most fabulous place on earth.

This voyage is almost at an end now. Tomorrow morning we dock in Ushuaia. We'll miss life on board and all the friends we've made. Our friends from kayaking and some of our fellow passengers. We've exchanged email addresses with John and Marlene, a very sociable Dutch couple with whom we've spent many an amusing evening over dinner whilst on board. I was initially attracted to John's deeply politically incorrect sense of humour when, at our hotel on the eve of departure, a very dry rather humourless box ticking pre embarkation meeting was taking place. At one point the rather uninspiring speaker was checking that passengers had not been to areas affected by various tropical diseases recently. At which point John, beer glass in hand, said out of boredom in rather a loud voice "Am I the only one with ebola?" We spent the rest of the rather dull briefing snickering like four naughty school children. It was great. Since that moment we've all been great friends. I've no doubt we'll stay in touch.

I'm going to sign off now to go and get some air on deck, as we are in the Drake Passage heading north and the ship is starting to roll on those large swells I was talking about... It's time to speak to the albatrosses.

CHAPTER 7
DECEMBER - YUCATAN PENINSULA, MEXICO

The British winter is a terrible thing. Trees shed their leaves, birds migrate, certain more intelligent types of mammals hibernate. Faced with the deep freeze back in England, Jan and I have no intention of returning home any time soon. We have capriciously abandoned dreary old monochrome Britain for the seductive promise of warm sunshine and the lively culture of Mexico. Having stored our down jackets and other cold weather gear at an airport hotel in Mexico City, we are left with lighter rucksacks containing warm weather clothing and other gear. When you travel with a mixture of cold and hot weather gear, it is essential to find conveniently located hotels willing to store the unwanted gear pending your return. A hotel at an airport which you fly into and out of is ideal.

If you paid too much attention to the BBC News you might be forgiven for thinking that any traveller to Mexico would most likely be dead within a couple of days of arrival at the hands of one drug cartel or another. Whilst I accept that drug related crime is indeed a serious problem, particularly near the US border, the sensationalist media sadly leave out a few rather important details.

Mexico has a particularly warm and courteous people, a pleasant sunny climate even in the winter, great food and even better beer. I am not talking about Sol and Corona lager, which they sell in trendy London bars at ridiculous prices, but here there are dark beers good enough to compete for top prizes at UK real ale festivals. Furthermore, the country has a rich pre and post colonial history which you can freely experience by visiting its magnificent archaeological sites and colonial towns. Its sheer size and geographical diversity lends itself to a wide variety of outdoor activities. Add to this the fact that Mexican prices are about one third of what things would cost in the UK and it doesn't sound like such a bad place to spend the winter after all. Unless you're a drug dealer. It's a pity they don't tell you all this on the dreaded News at Ten!

Our first stop in Yucatan, once we'd escaped the high rise horrors of Cancun, was the old Spanish colonial city of Valladolid, founded by the conquistadors and their Franciscan cronies in the 1550's. Though technically a city in that it is both ancient and has a cathedral, it really is not that big and has much more the feel of a provincial market town. Boasting a truly wonderful central plaza, impressive cathedral and monasteries and many superbly preserved low rise colonial buildings, the place oozes history and Old World culture. La Plaza Mayor is a great place to wander around aimlessly, particularly in the evening, with the cathedral illuminated beyond the trees and with many Mexicans of all ages clearly enjoying the outdoor moment, perhaps aided by a band playing lively local music. The sort of place that effortlessly holds you in its seductive embrace before you have to reluctantly prize yourself away to return to your hotel room. Much better than watching television with the central heating going full blast!

However, we didn't come to Valladolid to just admire the scenery. We stayed for a week during which we spent a couple of hours each morning revising our rusty Spanish. Spanish is a great language in that it is easy to learn and pronounce and is the language of the whole of Central and South America, apart from Brazil. So the effort made to learn it in one country is an investment repaid many times over in terms of subsequent visits to some of the most interesting countries in the world. The accents and dialects vary of course but it's the same language. The locals appreciate you making the effort and you can share the odd joke with them. Speaking English in a loud voice may work in the tourist centres but if you want to get off the beaten track you need at least some proficiency in the language of Cortes. Besides, how else would you truly get to a country's heart and soul?

Yucatan is world famous for its cenotes. Cenotes are underground limestone sinkholes. There are only about six thousand cenotes in the world and two thousand five hundred of them are found here in Yucatan. The Yucatan Peninsula itself is a giant slab of limestone with no visible rivers above ground. All water flows underground from cenote to cenote, carving its way through the soft rock. These underground wells were a key source of water for the early Mayans, allowing their great city states to flourish. They were also a place where their rain god Chaac dwelt and were considered the entrance to the underworld. The darker cenotes, where the ceiling has not yet collapsed, do actually exude a rather otherworldly aura but are great places to relax and cool off in the heat of the dry season. In the afternoon after Spanish classes we would hire bikes and head off to a cenote with our swimming gear.

We were not the only people on bikes. Many Mexican pilgrims had travelled far and were now noisily returning on bikes and on foot, trailing banners, with back up vehicles noisily blaring horns, in order to be back in their home town to celebrate the birthday of the Virgin Mary on the 12th December. Whilst out cycling, I had to resist the temptation to overtake some of them and quickly put distance between us. I didn't want to upset the pilgrims or, even worse, bring about divine retribution. I think in actual fact it would be quite difficult to offend people here because in Mexico, as they say, " Todo se puede". Anything goes! I find this very liberating.

Before leaving Yucatan we also dived two cenotes out of Tulum, starting with the straightforward Casa Cenote, which is completely open and linked to the sea. The beauty about cenotes is that their fresh water means that the visibility is much better compared to the ocean. Casa Cenote is no more than seven metres deep so is an ideal first dive. We'd not dived for a year and diving is very much a confidence sport. The water is a fabulous turquoise colour, fringed by mangroves, and it is a nursery for small fish. You can practise your buoyancy control, whilst looking up at the twisted tangle of mangrove roots reaching down from the surface like tentacles towards you.

The second cenote, Grand Cenote, was a stroll in the park for Jan but much more of a challenge for a fair weather tropical reef diver like myself. You actually enter a wonderful underground cavern in very clear visibility with ghostly limestone stalagmites and stalactites of great beauty illuminated in your torch's beam. Most of the time you can look back at the green haze of the open part of the cenote, which is very reassuring. However, before long things get much darker and in due course you come across a sign saying "Danger. Qualified cave divers only beyond this point". This was unnerving for me and the point at which I was able to quickly turn and retrace my steps along the guide rope, heading with a growing sense of relief towards the safety of that distant green and blue haze. I know my limitations. I'm happy to dive with enormous sharks but cave diving is really not my thing. I did however feel a real sense of achievement at having completed it.

After Yucatan we flew to Oaxaca, a much bigger city in southern Mexico but again with fine colonial heritage. We continue to study Spanish combined with some sightseeing. We shortly intend to visit the nearby great Zapotec ruins of Monte Alban, reputed to be one of the world's finest archaeological sites.

Yesterday was a great day. We struck out into the cordillera on a seventy kilometers organised mountain biking trip with Pedro Martinez, a very nice guy and minor local celebrity who used to ride for Mexico. It was wonderful to leave the city and taste the pure mountain air. Jan coped very well with some very draining cross winds but decided to climb into the support vehicle when faced with a straight ten kilometre steep uphill section of endless switchbacks. A very sensible decision on her part, but this left me facing an hour of climbing at altitude with an ex international five years my junior. We paused after half an hour for water but, when we got back on the bikes, Pedro ominously uttered the words "Ahora vamos a trabajar" ("Now we are going to work"). He was not joking and I found myself in desperate rearguard action just to stay on his wheel as his smooth cadence propelled him ever upwards. Still, I managed to stay there by virtue of dogged resolve and the view from the top was almost worth it. Needless to say, I slept extremely well last night!

As if that wasn't enough, we are now signed on with Pedro for a crazy four day mountain biking trip starting on 26th December. This will take us up and over the high sierra to 2,000 metres above sea level, before plunging down dramatically to the Pacific coast at Puerto Escondido, a seaside resort to the east of Acapulco. The plan is to stay in local mountain villages untouched by internet and telephone in accommodation which has been described to us by Pedro as being "Muy rustico". I doubt a word of English will be uttered during the entire trip. So much for the luxury of Acapulco! We'll keep you posted. Wishing you all a Happy Christmas.

CHAPTER 8
DECEMBER - LA VUELTA A PUERTO ESCONDIDO

We hope you are well, surviving the winter and ready to be cheered up rather than depressed by our latest instalment.

Traditionally, Christmas in the UK is a time to increase your personal debt, argue with difficult relatives and take those first important steps towards obesity. When you are travelling it isn't much better. Hotels are always fully booked and even when you can find a room it will be at an inflated price. Many restaurants either close or similarly increase their prices. Museums and archaeological sites bolt their doors. In short, for the traveller Christmas and New Year are a pain for which you really need to plan ahead.

Our plan was to spend Christmas in the city of

Oaxaca in Southern Mexico. One bright spot is that on the 23rd December Oaxacans celebrate "La noche de los rabanos" ("Night of the radishes"). Only in Mexico could such an event occur. Any excuse for a fiesta. Oversized and inedible radishes are grown, finely sculpted and taken to the Zocalo, where they compete in an event that draws vast crowds of people. Of course, such a spectacle would not be complete without noisy fireworks. This year's winner was a brilliant and finely carved figure of legendary Mexican statesman and local boy Benito Juarez Radish…

On the 26th December our epic four day mountain biking trip started, when our ever enthusiastic and excellent guide Pedro picked us up at our hotel at eight thirty in the morning. The trip would prove tougher than anticipated.

Surely such a ride, starting at 1,600 metres above sea level in Oaxaca and finishing on the Pacific coast at Puerto Escondido at sea level, must be all downhill, right? However, such logic ignores the important fact that in between lies the over 2,000 metre high massif of the Sierra Madre Del Sur. During the first day, on reaching a vantage point, I casually asked Pedro which way was Puerto Escondido. When he pointed to the enormous mountain range seemingly stretching to infinity just ahead I thought he was joking. He was not!

The second miscalculation was to underestimate our companions. Pedro had mentioned that a Mexican family with two "Lads" would be joining us. For some reason I felt comforted, perhaps thinking the "Lads" would be quite young. However, he did not mention the fact that the eldest son, Sebastian, is twenty seven and a competition triathlete. His younger brother, Ernesto, is not much slower. Jorge, the father, is an experienced mountain biker with technique far superior to my own. Pilar, the mother, is a runner with a competitive attitude to whatever she happens to be doing. This was going to be hard work.

Each day was a tough fifty kilometre ride on dusty dirt tracks with over one thousand metres of ascent. Some of the hills were so steep your back wheel would spin helplessly under you if you got out of the saddle and the sharp downhill sections required maximum concentration. My mountain biking skills needed to improve and did so rapidly.

We stayed in very basic local mountain village accommodation which made for a very interesting cultural experience. One village had a wedding celebration going on which unfortunately kept everyone awake for most of the night.

The views of the Sierra Madre Del Sur throughout were just stunning, with each altitude zone having quite different vegetation and physical characteristics.

It certainly dwarfed the Surrey Hills. Box Hill takes me about seven and a half minutes to ascend. Certain hills here would take over an hour and, on a couple of occasions, I had to resist the temptation to flag down Alberto, our enthusiastic support vehicle driver, for a lift. Once, when I was having a bad day, he said he thought I looked "Mas muerto que vivo" ("More dead than alive").

On the fourth day it seemed like we would never reach the coast. Pedro tried to bolster our spirits, with the very best of motives, by constantly telling us that this was the "Ultima subida" ("Last hill"). After a while nobody believed him. There were mutinous rumblings that he was "Mentiroso" ("A liar") and at one point I thought a tired and overwrought Jan was about to deck him!

Puerto Escondido in Spanish means "Hidden port" but now, not only could we not see the port itself but the entire Pacific Ocean was proving elusive. Finally, we climbed yet another crest on the road and there it was, a blue haze on the horizon. Our Magellan moment! By now the cool high pine forests had given way to the steamy tropical climate of the coast and the last fifteen kilometres of the run in proved to be incredibly hot. We took on board vast quantities of water and fruit but I still managed to be very dehydrated the next day.

It was quite an achievement. Despite the challenges, everyone got on very well and the dynamics of the group made it a lot of fun. However, a similar future trip might prompt a long suffering Jan, who doesn't cycle that often, to petition for divorce on the grounds of my unreasonable behavior. I confess I would have little defence in court to allegations of such terrible abuse! A couple of days on the beach Acapulco style and a trip to Mexico City should hopefully placate her after her valiant efforts.

CHAPTER 9
JANUARY - A JOURNEY THROUGH MESOAMERICA

After the heroics on the Vuelta it was time to relax and soak up some of the culture that Mexico provides by visiting some of the impressive colonial cities and pre Columbian archaeological sites. Most educated people in the UK are aware of the great Mayan sites in the Yucatan peninsula, such as Chitchen Itza, Palenque and Uxmal. They are also aware of the Aztecs who were the rulers of Central Mexico when Cortes defeated Moctezuma in 1521. Perhaps what they don't realise is that these were just two of a whole host of pre Hispanic high civilisations in Central America that built great cities and shared common cultures. This geographical area is known as Mesoamerica. Starting with the early Olmecs, there were Zapotecs, Mixtecs, Toltecs, Huastecs and many, many more. Each civilisation tended to last only a few hundred years before its inevitable decline and fall.

Previous visits to the Mayan sites in Yucatan had whetted our appetite and on this trip we visited Monte Alban, El Tajin, Xochicalco and Tula, all very impressive sites. Fabulous and atmospheric though the sites are, you need to use a little historical imagination to envisage how things might have looked at their zenith. Try to imagine the stone walls with plaster on them, paint them in bright colours, maybe red and black. Add a few human figures...

Some of the museums housing the artefacts found on the archaeological digs are world class. The Museum of Anthropology in Jalapa (home of the pepper and known as "The London of Mexico" because of its frequent bad weather) has a separate section for each major Gulf civilisation. It boasts stunning works of art fashioned in pottery, stone, ceramics, jade, bone and other media. One of the star exhibits is a superbly crafted Olmec head weighing twenty tons, as big as some of the heads on Easter Island. It steadfastly returns your gaze as it impassively connects with you from across the centuries. For me the really striking thing about this collection is just how artistically talented the pre Hispanic civilisations were. There is a real joy and freedom of expression in much of their work. They captured facial expression in particular quite brilliantly.

Compare this with the colonial exhibits on display at other Mexican museums. They consist of a few oil paintings of stern looking conquistadors and shifty looking ecclesiastical types or a few tedious biblical scenes. It seems that, artistically at least, the pre Columbians were way ahead of the Spanish. Perhaps the conquest happened the wrong way round. However, the conquistadors had horses, better weaponry, smallpox and, of course, one thing in which they were world leaders, greed. I guess greed is the driving force behind all great empires.

I know you should never judge one period in history by the standards of another but it is hard to view the conquistadors with anything other than distaste. In Oaxaca I asked Hector, our Spanish tutor, what he felt Mexico had gained from three hundred years of Spanish rule. He pretended to be deep in thought before sarcastically raising one finger and saying "The language, nothing more". By way of contrast, Mexicans have a real pride in their pre colonial past and wandering around that museum in Jalapa it is easy to see why. Any people that buried their dead with "Sonrientes" (wonderfully expressive smiling clay masks) must be worth something. The Anthropology Museum in Mexico City is even better.

I don't totally agree with Hector. Some of the fine colonial buildings the Spanish left behind are amazing. The Spanish of course perfected the art of turning gold and silver into stone. As a result the Zocalo areas of Puebla or Mexico City are the equal of any great city centre in Europe. You can book into a decent hotel nearby, visit museums and galleries, pausing for coffee in the sunshine, without having to remortgage the house to do so.

Having considered Mexican history, it was time to enjoy some unique natural history. Valle de Bravo near Mexico City has some very special residents at this time of year. I'm sure you've seen the wildlife documentary. This is the place where millions of Monarch Butterflies go to overwinter having made one of nature's great migrations, a four thousand five hundred kilometre journey from the Great Lakes, on their fragile wings. After an hour of short sharp hiking, during which you gain five hundred metres of altitude, you arrive at the sanctuary at 3,000 metres above sea level. It is incredible to see the millions of brightly coloured Monarchs in thick clusters high in the pine trees. Once the sun warms their bodies a little, they beat their wings, taking to the air en masse in a truly mesmeric display. Nowhere else in the world will you see this spectacle but in Mexico. Sadly when they leave Mexico they will never return. They will lay their eggs up north for the next generation and only their descendants will return to these high altitude Mexican pine forests.

Before I go I need to make you aware of an addiction

I have acquired. Whilst in Puebla I naturally had to try Mole Poblano, Mexico's national dish. It is a delicious chocolate and chilli sauce, served as part of a main course, which, when mixed with a salsa picante, produces some exquisite tastes. Once I get home I will seek to kick the addiction and spend some time in rehab. I've even managed to get hold of some Mole powder and hope to smuggle it past UK customs. I hope you won't tip off the authorities.

May the gods (the pre Columbian ones!) accompany you.

CHAPTER 10
FEBRUARY - ALL ABOARD EL CHEPE TO THE COPPER CANYON

We hope this travelogue finds you well and coping admirably with the wet, cold and dark winter.

Following our archaeological tour of Central Mexico we flew north to Los Mochis on the Pacific coast. This is the starting point for an extraordinary railway journey. The Chihuahua al Pacifico Railroad (El Chepe) takes a leisurely and civilised thirteen hours to cover the four hundred miles from the Pacific to Chihuahua. It is a real engineering marvel in that from the town of El Fuerte to the top of the Copper Canyon at Divisadero it climbs more than two thousand metres using tunnels, bridges and endless switchbacks to cope with the inhospitable and rugged terrain.

Rather than starting in Los Mochis, we joined El

Chepe at the nearby tropical town of El Fuerte and, six hours and many fabulous panoramas later, alighted with our rucksacks at El Divisadero. The Barrancas del Cobre (Copper Canyon) is bigger by far than America's Grand Canyon and at El Divisadero you can stare down from the mirador into the vastness of the open canyon. The train stops for fifteen minutes here to allow awestruck passengers to disembark. However we were in no hurry and broke our journey by checking into a hotel only yards from the station, choosing a room with a balcony view. To be precise, our balcony was only two or three metres from the void. What a place to sip your Negra Modelo in the evening watching the colours of the canyon and the sky subtly change as the sun descends.

It is however a rather sad and melancholy place as here everything revolves around two train arrivals a day, the westbound train arriving at one in the afternoon and the eastbound one an hour later. Once the last El Chepe of the day boisterously sounds its klaxon and slowly pulls away, the sellers of food and local crafts all pack up their wares and go home, leaving you alone with your views. There is not a great deal to do here apart from strolling around the rim admiring the canyon and you find yourself going down to the station just to greet the train. I think in retrospect that a stay of one night would have been enough!

The next stop was Creel, a rough and ready logging town with cowboys driving pickup trucks and very much the feel of a wild west frontier town. One day there was a loose horse walking down the main street. Being in the same state as Ciudad Juarez, tourism here has really suffered from the drugs related violence but the town is trying to revive its fortunes by building a new airport. There was no chance of getting bored here if you like the great outdoors. At over 2,300 metres, mornings are cold in February but, when the sun inevitably comes out, the Sierra Tarahumara is a magical place of rugged mountains and scented pine forests and you naturally reach for your mountain bike, hiking boots or even the reins of your horse.

In Creel there is a local reserve maintained by the Raramuri Indians. These people fled up to the Copper Canyon in the sixteenth century to escape forced labour in Spanish silver mines. For a small fee you can take your mountain bike into their reserve to enjoy the excellent roads and trails. We hired bikes from the town and spent three days exploring the biking trails. By way of revenge, Jan took me horse riding and I have an injury to prove it. I'm not much of a horseman and whilst leading my horse down a slope on foot I kept him on too short a rope and the great clumsy beast accidentally stood on my foot! It's just bruising but I won't repeat that error in a hurry.

El Chepe finishes in Chihuahua and we spent a

couple of days exploring the city before going up to see Paquime, seat of arguably the only impressive pre Hispanic civilisation in northern Mexico. I was slightly disappointed not to see more small dogs with bulging eyes wandering around Chihuahua but a couple of good museums made up for it.

The Mexicans always enjoy a good revolution. We saw the cell where the revolutionary priest Miguel Hidalgo, who uttered the famous "Grito de independencia", spent his last night on earth before the Spanish executed him. Even better was the Casa de Francisco (Pancho) Villa, a much loved figure, with some fabulous photos of the 1910 revolution, including the actual bullet ridden car in which sadly he met his end. There is one great poster in which he is calling (Lord Kitchener like) for gringos to ride south with him for gold and glory. He was specifically looking for dynamiters, machine gunners and railroaders and promising weekly payment in gold. If interested you should report to Ciudad Juarez on the border by January 1915. I had to buy the t-shirt.

As our professions are not on Pancho's list, these particular gringos have decided not to ride with him but to carry on travelling after taking in some sunshine and warmth in Baja California. It has been cold up here in the north but worth the effort. We fly to La Paz tomorrow. Hasta luego gringos.

CHAPTER 11
FEBRUARY - WHALES AND SHARKS IN THE SEA OF CORTEZ

Apart from the warmth, our main purpose in visiting the Sea of Cortes was wildlife viewing. Seeing wildlife can of course never be guaranteed but it is possible to considerably enhance your chances by being in the right place at the right time. In Yucatan for example Isla Holbox is a great place to see Whale Sharks but not at this time of year. In the Sea of Cortes, February is a good time to see Whale Sharks and a visit to nearby Magdalena Bay will pretty much guarantee an encounter with a Pacific Grey Whale.

Whale Sharks are the biggest sharks in the world but harmless to people as they eat only plankton. You cannot dive with the sharks as, strange as it may seem for such large creatures, exhaled bubbles from scuba tanks tend to frighten them. Snorkelling therefore is the only option. The boat positions itself in the shark's path and, at the right moment, you have to slither into the water rather than jump, so as not to spook it. Our juvenile shark at six metres was comparatively small (they can grow as large as twenty metres) but it still looked huge in the water. As it was filter feeding it stayed on the move and, even though I was finning flat out, I struggled to keep up with it. I took special care to avoid its enormous tail which could easily accidentally knock you out. At one point the great shark turned and came directly underneath me, giving me a superb view of its huge gaping mouth only a few feet away. This was the only Whale Shark I have ever seen in over twenty years of scuba diving but it was certainly worth the wait. When he had gone, we both clambered back on the boat smiling broadly. What a fantastic experience.

The final wildlife encounter was with Pacific Grey Whales on the Pacific side of the Baja Peninsula. Having spent three days kayaking and being pestered by Sea Lions around Espiritu Santu Island, we went up to Magdalena Bay, where these impressive migratory whales congregate in large numbers at this time of year to mate and for the females to give birth. You are not allowed to get in the water with them or kayak amongst them but you can observe them from small boats. Most encounters are fairly brief as these enormous creatures are intent on other matters. However some of them are very friendly and inquisitive and swim under the boat, coming up close enough to touch. It's an amazing natural spectacle. It's not every day you get so close to such a massive wild creature.

Just before picking up our gear and flying out of Mexico City we visited a wonderful nearby two thousand year old archaeological site, Teotihuacan. It is a site on a truly massive scale. Our usual strategy of staying over locally and being the first through the turnstiles worked a treat. As we arrived, the bleary eyed merchandise sellers were still setting up their stalls. On a distinctly chilly early Monday morning (Mexico City is at over 2,000 metres) we sat alone on the top of the Templo Del Sol, at seventy metres a massive structure and the third largest pyramid in the world. We were the only people up there for a good forty five minutes as the sun cast long shadows over this magnificent monument and struggled to burn off the early morning mist. It is a pre Aztec site and the Aztecs themselves were said to have been in awe of the people whose high civilisation had been capable of constructing such a place. This place is in my view rightly considered to be perhaps the most impressive pre Hispanic site in the whole of Central America. If you ever come to Mexico City you simply have to see it.

Our time in Mexico is sadly coming to an end. It has been fabulous. This time there is no repetition of that all too familiar sinking feeling at the end of a great holiday. We are heading east, not to the UK though. Madagascar and South Africa are calling us.

CHAPTER 12
MARCH - IN SEARCH OF THE GIRAFFE NECKED WEEVIL

Madagascar has been on our bucket list for as long as I can remember. It separated from mainland Africa in the age of the dinosaurs, a massive mysterious tropical island buffeted by the cyclones of the Indian Ocean. Because of the length of time of its isolation (one hundred and twenty five million years) life here has evolved in its own inimitable way. Like Galapagos, it is a crucible of evolution containing much flora and fauna not found anywhere else. This makes it important for the whole world. Of course it's most famous sons are its lemurs, an ancient primate order distinct from and much older than monkeys and mankind.

The only question was how to plan the trip. Given we were going to South Africa anyway it made perfect sense to fly to its capital city, Tana, direct from Johannesburg which is only three hours away. March in South Africa would mean the rainy season in Madagascar and so long as we packed waterproofs there would be far fewer tourists around leading to a more intimate and exclusive experience.

That was the theory but in practice things went a little less smoothly. We had already had to postpone the trip twice before our big trip due to an airline strike and family health issues. Were we fated never to arrive? It certainly seemed that way as we sat on the tarmac at Johannesburg's OR Tambo International Airport and the pilot informed us with exasperation that the second aircraft, to which we had all just been transferred, now had technical problems of its own. In the end we did arrive safely in Tana but three hours late. On the way to our hotel the heavens opened with a vengeance, bringing the dense rush hour traffic to a complete standstill and leaving us in no doubt that this was indeed the rainy season.

Thankfully the following day dawned bright and sunny and we optimistically headed east through the rice paddies for four hours on the main road from Tana to Andasibe and Mantadia National Park. Our luck appeared to have changed and maybe we would get to see our lemurs after all.

The literature from our Tana based tour company

promised the possibility of seeing all manner of wondrously named specimens of Darwinian evolution such as the Giraffe Necked Weevil, the Diademed Sifaka, the Leaf Tailed Gecko and the Madagascan Painted Frog. Michel, the very helpful owner of 'Ortours', had booked us into some top end hotels with breakfast and we had at our disposal Fali, a safe driver with a sunny disposition in charge of a four wheel drive vehicle. Such a vehicle could be very useful in the rainy season. We would be responsible for paying for local National Park guides and picking up the tab for our lunches, dinners and beer. We had specifically asked Michel to design a week long trip to maximise wildlife viewing opportunities, at the same time as minimising road travel on the country's rather shaky road system given the season.

Our first encounter with lemurs took place on Lemur Island, a private reserve run by a local hotel. It was effectively a refuge for lemurs previously kept as pets and so habituated to people. Though we had been told they were friendly this proved to be a massive understatement as within seconds of landing on the island Jan had about three of these impossibly cute and adorable creatures perched on her shoulders and head. This virtual petting zoo was not precisely what we had in mind when we came to Madagascar. I must be honest though, we both had grins on our faces as broad as Cheshire cats as the two types of lemurs ran riot all over us in search of food. We were told that though lemurs don't like water, if they were unhappy they could leave the island as the crossing was a very narrow one. Not expecting such a close encounter we had packed the wrong camera. One with a large telephoto lens!

The next day we were introduced to John, our local National Park guide for the next few days. It was immediately obvious he was a gifted spotter. He amazed us by having Fali stop the car when he had unbelievably just picked out a Pygmy Chameleon, the smallest in the country and a master of disguise, on a bush at the side of the road. I struggled to see it even after he had pointed directly at it for several seconds from about a foot away. Where is it?

John is also a serious and passionate environmentalist with no time for the petting zoo of Lemur Island, dismissing it as a lemur prison and a place where the more superficial and empty headed tourists go to see a tame lemur, tick the box and head for the beach. He singled out the Chinese and French as particularly culpable in this regard!

Things lightened up a little when we mentioned we were serious hikers. He seemed to approve and promptly took us on a five hour spotting hike through Mantadia National Park to see some real wildlife. We would have to brave the numerous leeches and mosquitoes and do things the hard way under him. But he promised us the rewards would be worth the sacrifices and effort and we would experience the wonders of his country's stunning wildlife in its natural environment, its behaviour unaffected by our curious eyes.

I immediately kicked myself for wearing shorts rather than long trousers tucked into socks as the mosquitoes gleefully went to work, rising up from the spongy forest floor like a single living organism. If you lingered in one spot for too long their accomplices the leeches would quickly find you and burrow straight through your socks in search of warm blood. The first you would know about it was when you noticed a crimson patch on your sock.

The hike was fantastic. We had the whole national park to ourselves and John was right. To see a wild troupe of Indri, the largest lemur, moving effortlessly through the forest and vocalising at full volume is an experience not easily forgotten. They are so comfortable thirty metres up in the canopy of their ancient tropical hardwood forest home, their deafening and haunting calls echoing defiantly far and wide.

Long may these calls continue. The Indri always die in captivity. They either live in their forests in liberty or not at all. If we kill their forests we kill them. They do things on their own terms. Darwinists would probably criticise their lack of adaptability but I think they are rather magnificent. As we squinted our eyes at the canopy, straining our sore necks, we weren't laughing uproariously like we did at Lemur Island. However the experience felt right, better, perhaps more appropriate to the twenty first century.

Over the next few days John took us into his rainforest many times both during the day and at night. At night the smaller lemurs and chameleons come out under cover of darkness. The lack of other tourists made it a very exclusive experience. We saw many species of lemur, chameleons, countless birds, tree frogs, spiders, snakes and snails. Left to our own devices we would hardly have spotted any of it.

I always think this sort of tourism is the way forward. The local people are given a direct economic incentive to conserve wildlife by the creation of jobs in tourism and related fields. Over the years the vast majority of the country's forests has been cleared due to the rising population and consequent need to engage in slash and burn agriculture in order to provide food. National Parks offering paid work to local people provide a beacon of hope amidst this depressing backdrop.

I also think that Lemur Island does perhaps have a role to play as not everyone has the fitness, resolve, madness or even inclination to plough through the rainforests for hours on end. We need as many people on board as possible if the conservation message is to be successful.

We are off to Tana now. It was sad to say goodbye to the sleepy little village of Andasibe with its friendly people and amazing wildlife. No doubt the big city will seem irksome after all that beauty. At least our hotel in Tana has one of the best restaurants in the country, a wonderful legacy of French colonial power. By contrast the Brits could only bequeath boring concepts like democracy to their former colonies. After days of mediocre food in Andasibe, it's pretty clear to me at this very moment which legacy was more important! No need to worry about snails or frogs' legs though. When the French told the Malagasy that these things were good to eat they were met with a polite but resolute 'Really?'

We fly to Johannesburg tomorrow and then on to Cape Town.

CHAPTER 13
APRIL - ON TOUR IN THE WESTERN CAPE

I've done some pretty daft things in my time and what I was presently engaged in had to be right up there in the all time hall of fame. We were on a shark diving boat off Gansbaai, virtually at the southern tip of Africa, a place known as the Great White Shark capital of the world. More specifically I was in a cage attached to the side of the boat, peering through my mask into the murky water. The pitching of the boat in the light swell was starting to give me sea sickness and the seven millimetre wetsuit I was wearing seemed to afford scant protection from the distinct chill of the Agulhas current.

I was thinking to myself "Why on earth am I doing this?" The visibility in the shallows at this time of year was poor, perhaps a foot, two at most. In order to see the massive shark underwater he would have to swim right up and put his nose against the cage. Meanwhile the crew were patiently trying to lure the distant fins towards us with a decoy board in the silhouette of a seal and fish bait. After twenty five minutes of feeling cold and seasick I'd really had enough.

Suddenly we saw the fin of a three metre plus Great White heading our way. I tracked its movements on the surface and, with mask on, suddenly ducked down under the water. Then a massive head bristling with large serrated teeth stopped in front of us, checking us out. With heart racing, I practically jumped out of my skin, visibly flinching back from such a magnificent predator. I think everyone else in the cage must have reacted in the same way judging by the shouts of "Wow", "Bloody hell" and other choice expletives once he had gone. What a creature!

These encounters are great fun but I'm not going to pretend that there is much scientific purpose behind all this thrill seeking other than a percentage of the takings going to White Shark conservation (tagging and monitoring of movements etc). On board is an interesting marine biologist and volunteers identify the sharks encountered by their distinct markings. We met Peter and the inappropriately named Little Rosie. Anyone can do the trip and though it is called a dive absolutely no diving experience is necessary. All you need is a wetsuit and mask.

Scarcely had we completed our shark experience than

we embarked on a six day self guided cycling trip through the Overberg, a little touristed area to the east of Gansbaai. Most people pass through it on their way to the Garden Route. It is a tough uncompromising place of high veld and farmland but with a harsh and rugged beauty to set the heart racing. The mountain biking trip was a real challenge as we had to contend with a combination of blisteringly dry heat, little availability of water, strong cross winds and poor heavily corrugated unpaved roads which easily turn to mud after rainfall. The Overberg threw all these things at us over the course of the week. It's the sort of place where you need a company that offers good reliable backup and support. It's a pity the company we employed for this purpose didn't offer any of these things but that's another story and at least we survived! They did at least compensate us financially, taking steps to ensure no repetition. They therefore remain nameless! Such a shame as the walking tour they organised for us around the vineyards and into Stellenbosch had been such a success.

South Africa has, of course, come a long way since the dismantling of Apartheid. If you're in any doubt about the evils of that particular system of racial separation I'd recommend a visit to the Apartheid Museum in Johannesburg. It's a brilliant museum but pulls no punches in its graphic harrowing displays, photographs, films and archives. It succeeds in creating such an atmosphere of menace and stifling oppression that in the end I found myself delighted just to be outside in the warm sunshine, breathing deeply the clean air and relieved that this recent dark chapter has been consigned to history. I'm a fairly privileged white Englishman. I'm not sure how I'd have felt if I had visited as a black person. Maybe everyone needs to go and see it.

South Africa is of course currently pursuing a gradual approach to material equality, which has got to be better than Zimbabwe's madness, but I can't help thinking that things need to progress a little quicker. The disparity in wealth between blacks and whites is still shocking to a European. White people often seem to enjoy a wonderful outdoor lifestyle in large houses with plenty of space, better than in the UK really. By contrast, some of the shacks by the side of the motorway as you drive into Cape Town are quite shocking. I'm told that more and more blacks are entering the ranks of the professional middle classes and that there is in force a policy of positive discrimination to favour black applicants for jobs. I hope these measures have the desired effect, but sooner rather than later. On the plus side there is a real "Go ahead", "Can do" mentality in the people which is very positive and refreshing to see. They just get on with things and have none of the unfortunate sense of entitlement which you see in certain individuals in Europe. I wish them well.

Given its wealth disparity South Africa has a bit of a reputation for crime. We never once felt threatened. It's true that we don't spend much time hanging around big cities at night, or flashing expensive possessions around or appearing obviously lost. We always get cash out of ATMs first thing in the morning when the thieves and pickpockets are still in bed! I think as long as you are careful you'll be fine.

However a vast amount of money is spent on keeping properties and individuals safe and secure. Security really is big business here. I think though that the perception or fear of crime here is arguably worse than the crime itself. Nobody wants anything to happen to a close family member because they didn't spend money on making their property secure. You are told never to stop for hitchhikers by the roadside. But is the beautifully dressed middle aged black lady on her way to church when there's no public transport really going to pull a knife on you and drive off in your hire car? Sometimes I suggested we might stop and do just that. Jan said the guidebook really didn't recommend it. I all too willingly agreed and then felt bad about it. We both did. We almost felt we were part of the system of oppression. It's that fear thing again.

We've really enjoyed the Cape and will certainly be coming back to South Africa. It will be a great winter destination in the future and, being pretty much due south of the UK, the time difference is minimal so there's no jetlag to worry about. Having served our apprenticeship as travellers in the Cape we'll be happy to go elsewhere in this wonderful country with more confidence now.

Shortly we'll be leaving South Africa but as I write, the sun is shining and we have a great view of Cape Agulhas, a stormy and rugged place where the Atlantic and Indian Oceans meet, from our balcony. There are two glasses on the table and a suitably chilled bottle of the excellent local Viognier sits in the fridge. There are worse things in life.

CHAPTER 14
MAY - CAMPING ON THE ROOF OF AFRICA

This update comes to you from Ethiopia where we have just completed three weeks of travel. Ethiopia is a hot, dusty, noisy, impoverished and overpopulated African country. Travel is challenging. The food makes English pub fare seem like a sophisticated international cuisine. Hotels are generally of a poor standard and not good value for money. Furthermore Ethiopia has recently increased the admission fee to its historical monuments by several hundred percent but without any corresponding benefit to foreign visitors. Why then bother? I could lie to you and say that we were inspired by its rich history and culture and the warmth of its people. However our real reason for coming here is that it is the only place in the world where you can see the Gelada Baboon, a powerful golden maned primate that lives in large social groups at high altitude and feeds on grass.

Ever since seeing a David Attenborough documentary I have wanted to sit on a mountain top as part of a baboon troupe and watch the sun come up over the Escarpment, a huge flat four thousand metres high lump of rock at the head of the Rift Valley that falls away vertically a thousand metres to the valley floor beneath. Just as people go to Rwanda to see Mountain Gorillas we had come to Ethiopia to trek with the Gelada.

Our five day camping trek in the Simien Mountains had cost us one thousand US dollars in total. This seems like quite a lot of money till I tell you of the manpower involved to look after only two people. We had a general guide, a local guide, a scout, a cook, an assistant cook and three mule handlers. If you think the above is rather excessive you would not be wrong. It seems like the sort of job creation scheme of which even a 1970s British trade unionist would have been proud. However, having paid over our money it was up to 'Explore Abyssinia', our local operator, to decide how to spend it.

During the trek we would carry only a day sack, the rest of our gear transported by mule. All the mules here are called either "Bullit" or "Bullu" depending on their sex. On arrival at the evening campsite we would find our tent pitched as if by miracle and a welcome cup of tea awaiting us. What luxury. Our two guides were both educated and knowledgeable but both cooks in dire need of retraining. I will sadly never forget the soggy steamed vegetable sandwiches they delighted in producing for lunch. Most of these went to the local ravens. I think to be fair to them that vegetarianism is a concept not really practised nor understood in Ethiopia. Not only in Ethiopia either. I was fine with the injera, a spongy flatbread served with a sauce on top everywhere you go. It's the national dish. Jan couldn't stand it though!

The compulsory scout Mohammed was the most interesting member of our mini expedition. A tall imposing bearded figure wearing traditional turban and blanket, he was sixty three but still very fit. With a rifle from the Great War and twelve bullets he would bring up the rear of the group, a reassuring figure as leopards and hyenas lurk in the mountains. Tough as old boots, he carried only a blanket for the cold nights and a small bag from which occasionally he would produce a Koran. He could not speak a word of English nor I Amharic but I cannot recall instantly liking someone quite so much in a long time.

The trek was stunning as we moved up the Escarpment. It was stiflingly hot during the day with few trees for shelter but freezing at night due to the altitude. We stopped at a local village of people actually living within the National Park. There is currently a move to relocate these people from the

Park where they have always lived but both Emperor Selassie and the Communist Derg had tried and failed in the past. The problem is that the land they cultivate is each year encroaching further into the Park, driven by an ever increasing population. Given that the Park is not that big to start with you wonder about its long term viability should this trend continue.

In the short term at least, the wildlife is safe and we were able to spend some quality time with our beloved Gelada. Sometimes we were able to approach to within a few feet of them as they warmed up on the edge of a precipice in the early morning sun. We observed many aspects of their behaviour from feeding to grooming to inter male rivalry to bedding down on steep cliffs for the night. The males have large teeth but are not aggressive to people, though they prefer white people to Ethiopians. This is not racism but simply reflects the fact that many years ago the locals hunted them. Now killing a baboon carries a ten year sentence but the real reason for the change in attitude is not the threat of punishment but the tourist dollars they bring in.

The often hectic scenes at the campsites were straight out of the sort of Ethiopia that dwells in our imaginations. Goatherds as young as five or six desperately trying to control their recalcitrant flocks with sticks and stones. Cooks noisily chasing off mischievous groups of local kids dressed in rags.

Colourfully clad highlanders driving their precious livestock down to distant villages in the fading evening light where they are safe from nocturnal predators. It could only have been Ethiopia.

Having achieved honorary membership of the Gelada troupe, we then embarked on a second trek but, rather than camping, we stayed in local villages, which was culturally very interesting. We also visited the famous rock hewn churches of Lalibela, the castle at Gondar and Lake Tana's monasteries. We found Lalibela's Christian Orthodox churches carved into the hillside fascinating but did get a bit fed up having our tickets checked repeatedly. This in addition to raising the ticket prices so sharply is not a good way to build up a tourist industry.

The local people in the countryside outside of Addis obviously don't see too many foreigners. Sometimes they have a strange way of greeting you. They point at you and with a broad smile say "You...you, you, you, you, you"! Once we had a beer in a very basic shack near the market whilst trekking through a larger town in the mountains. They served it to us in a tin can. The people are very curious and friendly. Nothing goes to waste. Once you've finished with a plastic bottle a local kid will be miraculously at hand in the middle of nowhere to take it off your hands. I expect it will be reused for storing water. We try not to create too much plastic waste, treating the tap water instead with iodine before drinking it.

Ethiopia can be very hard work and sometimes in a moment of weakness you find yourself asking if it is really worth it. It is, however, fascinating and of course it is to see cultures that are totally different from your own that you travel. Still, we've got some great photos and memories of the Gelada and that is why we really came.

The other day I was bemused to see an Ethiopian cycling along in traffic with a sheep tied to his back. Strangely enough the expression on the sheep's face indicated that it was enjoying the experience, as if it was something that it had always wanted to do but had never had the opportunity! Time to leave I think!

CHAPTER 15
JUNE - SRI LANKAN DIARIES

Our next destination as we made our way eastwards was going to be either India or Sri Lanka. Whilst briefly travelling in India previously, we had found it quite hard work and this in the end tipped the scales in Sri Lanka's favour. We decided rightly or wrongly that Sri Lanka would probably give a similar sort of cultural experience to India but with rather less hassle.

Our first port of call, having left excess gear near Colombo, was Mirissa, a minor outpost of mass tourism. This is the sort of place where pale overweight ghosts, temporary refugees from northern Europe, come to snatch a week of tropical warmth in order to recharge their bodies and minds after the stresses of the modern workplace. If there is plenty of blubber on display on the beaches then there is even more to be found out at sea. In whale watching terms Mirissa is fast acquiring the reputation of the best place in the world to see the iconic Blue Whale. This is why we had come.

The Blue Whale, at up to thirty metres long and weighing in at up to one hundred and seventy tons, is the largest creature ever to have lived on Planet Earth. No land or sea dinosaur was bigger. It was extensively and brutally hunted by the ruthless whaling industry in the 1960s until at the last hour it received protection from the International Whaling Commission as an endangered species. It is thought there may be fewer than five thousand left in all the oceans of the world and it has become a defining symbol of the worldwide conservation movement. If we can't save the Blue Whale what can we do?

Our organised whale watching trip was certainly not an easy coastal jaunt. The sturdy boat headed due south from Mirissa Harbour at seven in the morning into the heavy swells of the Indian Ocean, maintaining its course for three hours. Within less than half an hour some people could be seen fumbling with sick bags or with their heads over the side in that unmistakable way. On the way out the wind was on our beam, making the boat roll from side to side in exaggerated fashion. For the return journey the wind, by way of further torment, had swung round and freshened, forcing us to punch our way home directly into heavy seas.

After five hours we had not even seen a solitary

porpoise for all our sacrifice. Then when everyone had given up hope (in more ways than one) one of the crew spotted the trademark spout. We approached the leviathan in a roundabout way (whale watching regulations prohibit steering directly at a whale) and were able to observe a fifteen metre Blue Whale on the surface. It's odd that he looks grey on the surface but when slightly below the water he has that distinct blue tinge for which presumably he was named by whalers. He stayed with us for only a few minutes and then, tiring of our attentions, his huge tail fluke came up and he was gone into the deep. We waited for fifteen minutes, all eyes scanning the horizon, to see if he would resurface nearby but it was not to be and we never saw him again.

What an amazing experience. How many people do you know, other than professional wildlife photographers, who have seen a Blue Whale? This was yet another item on the bucket list to be firmly crossed through. At this rate we'd be running out of things to do!

Wildlife sightings can never be guaranteed however and luck tends to even itself out over the longer term. This we found out in Yala National Park where we went in search of the park's famous but elusive leopards. Though we enjoyed the full day's safari and saw much other interesting wildlife in this famous Sri Lankan coastal reserve, the leopards themselves remained elusive. Not to worry. There's always another day.

After a scenic rail journey up through the tea plantations of the Hill Country from Ella to Kandy, we decided to immerse ourselves in Sri Lankan history and culture for a while. We headed north and visited three World Heritage sites in Polonnaruwa, Sigiriya and Dambulla.

Polonnaruwa was, in the Middle Ages, the capital city of Sri Lanka and today you can cycle round its atmospheric crumbling ruins. As usual we made an early start ahead of the tourist hordes and found ourselves the first people at the ancient Quadrangle that day and for forty five minutes or so we owned the ancient city just as surely as any Sinhalese king ever did. The buildings, made with a brick core and finished in stucco (plaster), are in various stages of decay but in one temple, the Image House, you could clearly pick out the facial expressions of the people in the frescoes. They looked very much like you and me.

Dambulla is an ancient rock temple hewn from the underside of a huge granite boulder. Many Buddha images, including huge reclining Buddhas, have been fashioned out of the rock with colourful frescoes painted on the walls and ceilings. It is still used as a place of worship and the presence of local people praying, chanting and burning incense in the subterranean early morning gloom really enhanced the atmosphere of this very special place. Needless to say, we were the first through the turnstiles and were able to position ourselves in such a way as to discreetly observe proceedings at our leisure. Not too close to be a nuisance to the worshippers but close enough to see what was going on. Hats off. No photos during the ceremonies. Of course before photographing people you should always ask their permission first.

Finally, Sigiriya is a massive three hundred and seventy metre high boulder soaring imposingly above the surrounding rain forests and wetlands. On the flat top are the fortress like ruins of a monastery or palace (there is debate about its true purpose). Half way up are the most amazingly preserved frescoes, the gallery accessed via a precarious looking metal spiral staircase. At the base of the rock are exquisitely landscaped gardens. Starting at seven thirty in the cool of the morning the climb itself was straightforward. The views from the top are superb over the whole of the surrounding area, with the added archaeological dimension of the question posed by the ruins. This site has everything.

After all this dashing about the island in search of wildlife and culture we are feeling tired and will dedicate the last few days in the country to the mindless pursuit of relaxing on a beach. Mirissa, that minor outpost of mass tourism I mentioned earlier should do fine. With some spicy Sri Lankan curries washed down with plenty of "Lion", the local lager. We will be avoiding the local buses (mostly driven by homicidal maniacs) but will do one final rail journey. Rail journeys here are fun, fascinating and a great way to meet the local people. They are very friendly and helpful and mad on cricket. It's a pity I know so little about the game!

Before I go I must mention a wonderful flying experience we had here. I know you don't often hear the juxtaposition of these three words in the modern era of low cost airlines, enhanced airport security and screaming babies on flights. However if you think that the days of glamour in the airline industry are long gone you'd actually be wrong.

The second time we visited Mirissa we took the seaplane from a lake just outside Colombo to Lake Koggala, a large expanse of fresh water in the south. Having booked online we turned up one hour beforehand at a prefabricated building by the jetty to find there were only two other passengers. The seaplane was securely tethered to this jetty. Half an hour before the flight the captain turned up, bidding everyone a very cheery and sociable good morning. He and his co pilot then began a series of visual and manual checks on various parts of the sea plane, including turning the propellers by hand. This was very reassuring. Then friendly laid back cabin crew welcomed us aboard. Within about five minutes other employees had efficiently cast off the ropes and the captain was accelerating across the top of the water. After much fuss and vibration the seaplane eventually soared into the sky, turning to the south. The flight itself only lasted one hour. It was such a civilised experience from start to finish and not that expensive, almost like going back in time to the early glamour days of commercial aviation. Easyjet would do well to take note.

Lake Koggala itself is a military base. During the Second World War the RAF used to fly reconnaissance missions from the lake using Catalina flying boats. I know this because my stepmother Meg told me that her father was based here during the war. I remember one of her stories, which is rather sad. One of her father's senior officers returned from a long mission and flopped exhausted onto the boat carrying him ashore. Unfortunately, having fallen asleep, he left an arm trailing in the water. Suddenly a large crocodile seized him by the arm and dragged him under. His body was later recovered and the brave Squadron Leader was laid to rest in a military cemetery in Colombo. At the age of seventy eight Meg's father actually returned to the lake for the first time since the war. He also visited the military cemetery in Colombo. One can only imagine his feelings as he stood at the graveside and paid homage to his long fallen comrade.

Given Lake Koggala is still a military base the passengers were quickly and efficiently ushered off the base on arrival but not before I'd carefully scanned the banks for any descendants of the killer crocodile. I didn't see any. I even asked the friendly security guard, who didn't seem to know of them. Maybe they are all long gone.

CHAPTER 16
JULY - TREKKING IN NEPAL

In Nepal we decided to undertake two treks, one independently and the other guided. The second trek is described in the prologue to this book.

July is the rainy season in Nepal but because of the Himalayan rain shadow our trek to Upper Mustang was not affected. Our first trek to Helambu certainly was though. Though not ideal in that respect, it did however mean there were fewer trekkers on the trails and the valleys were in bloom. It would be practically impossible on an extended trip like this to have perfect conditions everywhere and we decided to make the most of it. We had top of the range waterproofs and we intended to get our money's worth out of them!

As steeped in history as the Kathmandu Valley is, the highlight of any trip to Nepal is a trekking expedition into the high Himalaya. To those who worship the mountains as we do, a trek in Nepal is every bit as important as the Haj to modern day Muslims or a pilgrimage to Canterbury Cathedral in Chaucer's time. It's something you should do at least once in your lifetime. The mountains here are certainly the highest and, in my opinion, the most beautiful in the world. There is no better feeling than padding around in your down jacket on a chilly morning in a Nepali mountain village, encouraging the sun to come up, with the aroma of a wood fire in your nostrils and prayer flags fluttering overhead. You just know that you are going to have an above average day.

Our fourteen day trek started at a trailhead only one hour's taxi ride from Kathmandu and would take us north towards the Tibetan border into the Helambu region. Further north comes a 4,600 metres pass, often closed to snow in winter, leading to the Hindu holy lakes of Gossainkund. From there it is easy to drop down into the Langtang valley with its wonderful views of Lantang Lirung, at 7,200 metres a true Himalayan giant.

Not only are the mountains sensational but the local Tamang culture is fascinating. The Tamang migrated from Tibet many generations ago bringing with them their Buddhist beliefs, making these mountains a deeply spiritual place. Everywhere there are gompas, chortens, chedis, mani walls and prayer flags. One lodge we stayed at had a small private monastery and another one was actually run by a lama, a Buddhist teacher. Lamas here are practical men of the world, farmers, lodge owners and husbands. No silly rules regarding celibacy and they actually make a contribution to society rather than being aloof and an economic burden on their people. This is the perfect pragmatic model for these largely subsistence farming mountain communities. Of course a simple prayer flag on the summit of a Himalayan pass far surpasses any cathedral or mosque ever built.

We opted to trek independently without guide or porter, given that maps are available and we don't mind packing a ten kilo rucksack. On route there are many tea houses and lodges to take tea, buy meals and stay at night so it is a pretty well worn track. The first two five or six hour days were tough given we had not trekked for a while but soon your muscles toughen up and, with the odd rest day thrown in, you become acclimatised to the altitude. With Acute Mountain Sickness (AMS) being potentially fatal, it is essential not to rush up the mountain and independent trekking gives more scope to stop and consolidate and really listen to your body than an organised trek with its schedules and deadlines set in stone.

By the time we reached the 4,600 metre Lauribina pass on the sixth day we were both feeling strong. Jan put in a wonderfully spirited performance to reach the prayer flags marking the top of the pass, with me carrying most of her gear. I loved every minute of it, the challenge, the magnificent scenery, the physicality of it all. The next day we scheduled a rest day to recover from the exertion and sat around drinking tea and eating Nak's cheese (the Nak being the female Yak). It is strong tasting but delicious.

However, every proper pilgrimage has an element of suffering. If the days are sublime, the long nights are freezing cold. The lodges are very basic with no electricity in the rooms. After dinner at six thirty you can eke out the time by chatting to other trekkers (if there are any) by the warm stove or read a book. By about eight o'clock with the fire dying back and all options exhausted you bow to the inevitable and go to bed. This can make for a long night if the altitude is preventing you from sleeping!

If you are impressed by all this please don't be. We met an Israeli-American couple who had just completed fifty five days of continuous trekking. It had become their way of life. Or the American lady who had just taken her eighty four year old mother over the 4,600 metres Lauribina Pass. They had porters to carry their gear but even so that is still an amazing achievement. The redoubtable lady confided in us that she thought this would be her last trek in Nepal! Or perhaps the Swiss guy who had jacked in his job as a lawyer, married a lama's daughter and was running a trekking lodge.

Less impressive were the two Israelis, probably having just completed military service, who had rushed up from the trailhead and when we met them on the pass one of them was staggering like a drunk, a classic symptom of AMS. I hope he recovered but that sort of arrogant stupidity has a habit of being severely punished in these high mountains. Altitude sickness is no respecter of youth or fitness levels and nobody can really predict how they will react. It helps to drink plenty of water to avoid dehydration, cut out alcohol and of course move up the mountain conservatively. You can take drugs such as Diamox but sometimes there are side effects and I tend not to need them in any case.

We're back in Kathmandu tomorrow. The ban on alcohol is mercifully at an end. I'm looking forward to celebrating with a curry and a few glasses of Everest, the rather good local beer. Much as I like Dhal Bhat, the lentil curry which is Nepal's national dish, I'm looking forward to a change. It's the perfect food for trekking with carbohydrate and protein, and the great thing is when you have finished they will come and fill up your plate again for free. Perfect when you are burning large amounts of calories at altitude but once you've stopped you could put on some serious weight. This is not a problem at the moment as we've both lost half a stone whilst trekking.

We particularly like the people of Nepal. They come from very tough and hardy mountain stock. Gurkhas, of course, have long been sought after by the Indian and British armies as they make exceptional soldiers. Yet Nepalis are also really nice friendly straightforward decent people despite their country being a poor one. You are not likely to see the latest consumer gadgets but there is more spirituality here and, in a strange sort of way, they actually seem a bit happier than people in the West. I would however like to see them close this wealth gap with the West, as other Asian countries such as Thailand have done in recent years.

After a few days exploring the Kathmandhu valley we shortly head over to Pokhara and then we'll undertake a guided trek to Upper Mustang. It will take us high up on the Tibetan Plateau and backwards in time. The flight into Jomsom where we start the trek should be interesting. We can't wait. But first a glass of Everest will go down really well.

CHAPTER 17
AUGUST - SAILING IN THAILAND

Though Thailand is very much a mainstream tourist destination, it nonetheless has many things going for it. It has a tropical climate, the people smile very easily and the food is world class. In all these respects it is the exact opposite of Britain! Its sunny tropical climate is a great place to go after the rigours of trekking in Nepal. Bangkok is the perfect travel hub, providing easy access to the rest of South East Asia.

I think we might have become rather bored if we had spent too much time on a beach, sipping Chang and Singha beer, but we were here for two reasons. Firstly, to acquire a sailing qualification which we hope later in the trip to rely on to charter a yacht in Tonga. Secondly, we will try to get off the beaten track on a self guided cycling trip in Chiang Mai Province in Northern Thailand. In the meantime, a few unambitious days on the beach at sea level would do us no harm at all after spending so much time at altitude. High altitude Nepalis are physiologically adapted to extracting oxygen from the thin air. Coming from a country where the highest mountain, Ben Nevis, is only a 1,300 metres pimple, we are certainly not.

The island of Phuket in Southern Thailand was our first destination where we would attempt to complete our Royal Yachting Association Day Skipper Practical qualification. This useful sailing qualification, combined with our Competent Crew certificate and the Day Skipper Theory we had both already completed online, would then enable us to charter yachts just about anywhere in the world in the future.

Thailand is the perfect place to do this course as it is classed as a tidal country, even though the tidal range on Spring tides, where the range is greatest, is only about two metres. We could have opted to complete the course in the Mediterranean but that sea is classed by the RYA as non tidal and a two day converter course would have been necessary to convert to a tidal qualification. We had considered Southampton as a venue for the course but not for long, as we had no desire to suffer sea sickness and hypothermia, when we could enjoy Phuket's tropical climate, easy way of life and excellent cuisine.

We are not the most experienced of sailors and I often think that the only way to really progress would be to own our own boat in the UK. However, I'm not sure we could put up with the weather and someone accurately said that owning your own boat is rather like standing in the shower tearing up twenty pound notes. As we don't sail that often it's much more cost effective for us to hire or charter a yacht when required.

When sailing, Jan and I normally have a boat all to ourselves and complement each other well. Jan is better on the technical side of things but can sometimes be a little fretful and cautious. I, on the other hand, have a certain self confidence around boats which is probably not justified or backed up by my limited experience. For this I blame my father Bill who earned a living as a captain in the Merchant Navy and then latterly as a river pilot. When I was young he was always taking myself and my younger brother Steve out on fishing and pilot boats. He even managed to secure me a job as a deck hand on the Firth of Forth between school and university. Here, under the benevolent tutelage of the pilot boat crew, as well as learning good seamanship, I fine tuned my drinking and swearing abilities to quite an impressive degree. When thirty years later I began to learn to sail these half forgotten qualities returned to stand me in good stead!

Our course boat in Thailand was a forty four footer with four cabins but with five students and an instructor on board for the five day course conditions were rather snug. Over the five days our instructor Simon, a very experienced sailor and excellent boat mechanic, kept us up to the mark in covering the RYA syllabus and I am delighted to say everyone passed the course.

Wind sadly was in short supply but the sailing grounds here are spectacular, characterised by warm tropical seas lapping against dramatic limestone karst formations. It is wonderful to clamber up on deck at about six in the morning with your pillow and bed sheet, still bleary eyed and sleepy, and just to sit propped up on deck with cup of tea in hand, contemplating the serenity and grandeur of these surroundings. At this point any annoyance at not having slept soundly in your own bed simply evaporates and all is well with the world.

It would be easy for the crew to fall out, being on a boat together continuously, occasionally sailing at night to satisfy the syllabus and sometimes not sleeping so well but in fact we all got on incredibly well. I think laughing at other people's and especially one's own stunningly inept acts of seamanship helped a great deal.

Some were straight out of the Costa Concordia manual of seamanship. On one occasion Mike fell out of his improvised hammock in the ship's bows, landing unhurt but with all the force of an Exocet missile. His partner Jo tried to drive the boat into the quayside during boat handling practice in a way that could only be described as like a Destroyer ramming a U boat. It was a good thing the jetty was absorbent plastic and not concrete. Determined not to be outdone, I myself tried to operate the winch but had forgotten the minor detail of first attaching the main sheet (rope) and couldn't understand why the sail was not coming in. I rightly received no end of ridicule for this! It was one of those days. But overall we did many more competent than incompetent things and were rightly awarded our certificates.

Sailors have long had a reputation for letting their hair down in port and I'm afraid to say we were no exception. With the ink only just dry on our beloved certificates, we headed off to the restaurant near the marina in high spirits and drank far too much. Mike and Jo are both ex pat Brits and could comfortably drink us under the table. There was much childish behaviour and I'm surprised we weren't asked to leave. Whenever one of us had to visit the bathroom his or her shipmates very helpfully shouted instructions such as "Starboard", "Hard to port" or "Full speed ahead" to guide us on our way. All very silly but good fun and at least the restaurant was empty by then.

Now we have our qualifications we can confidently look forward to sailing our charter yacht in Polynesia.

In the meantime, Northern Thailand beckons.

CHAPTER 18
AUGUST - CYCLING IN CHIANG MAI

Following a couple of days rest after our sailing course, we headed up to Northern Thailand to do our week long self guided cycling trip in the quiet countryside of Chiang Mai Province.

For an incredibly reasonable fifty pounds a day in total our operator gave us two sturdy well maintained Trek hybrid bikes with thick tyres, four panniers, helmets, an odometer and a comprehensive set of written instructions all linked to odometer readings. In addition, we received six accommodation vouchers to some comfortable resorts with swimming pools, including breakfast. We'd also had a very detailed briefing by Etienne, a very likeable and sociable gentleman who had learned his organisational skills in the Belgian military. The rest was up to us. What could possibly go wrong?

The daily distances were not great (between forty five to seventy five kilometres per day) but the terrain was often quite rough, with the odd mountain thrown in just for good measure. Etienne, owner of 'Click and Travel', had written his instructions in such a way as to avoid major roads where at all possible. These instructions were precise – "At 1.5 km turn right at the T junction. Follow the Ping River on your left. At 3.5 km pass Wat on your right..." All manner of symbols and abbreviations were used referenced to a glossary of terms. We quickly got into Etienne's mindset and after a while could confidently navigate with very few errors. We were also provided with a map and guidebook in case we managed to become hopelessly lost. If all else failed you could always phone Etienne up on the mobile he had kindly lent us, though to do so might smack of defeatism and would no doubt lead to a torrent of ridicule.

Cycling really is the best way to explore rural Thailand. On foot it would take too long, in a car rural life would whizz by in a meaningless blur. The pace of cycle travel also seems to match perfectly the pace of daily life in these tranquil Thai villages, where rice has been grown for millennia. Here there is so little motorised traffic that you need to precariously navigate a passage around one stubborn sleeping dog after another. Occasionally they suddenly liven up and, for a bit of sport, pursue you, whether out of boredom or perhaps to remind us that despite appearances they are still very much alive and kicking. In such situations it is better to ignore them and avoid getting them overexcited. This is more easily said than done when menaced by a large set of jaws! They tend to be worse when the temperatures are at their highest and they are feeling grumpy.

On our one week tour we passed a variety of landscapes from flat agricultural valleys bright green with rice and tropical fruit crops to wooded alpine villages. Everywhere there are peaceful wats and ancient chedis tended to by diligent saffron robed Buddhist monks. Some of the wats up in the mountain are fabulous and exude an aura of spirituality almost approaching that of Nepal. Out on the plains too there are some amazing sights. One day we passed a twenty metre high gilded statue of Lord Buddha, this colossus bestriding the rice fields like some great wonder of the ancient world. Thailand's Buddhist culture really is a fascinating one.

There was a great simplicity to life on the trip. You awake early with the sunlight and have breakfast at seven, starting out about eight as it is much easier to cycle in the cool of early morning. This is the best time of day and your legs seem to turn effortlessly. It's really worth banking a few miles at this time of day. All you need to worry about is following the instructions, deciding where to take a coffee break and selecting a suitable place for lunch. Perhaps buy some fruit or a few cans of Chang beer for later. What else would the panniers be for? You normally arrive at the resort about one in the afternoon, secure the bikes and jump in the pool. By now the sun is scorching so it is best not to attempt too much outdoors. Time for a good book. Cool Chang on the balcony about five thirty, dinner around six thirty. By nine in the evening you can hardly keep your eyes open, put down your book and sleep like a log. The following day this freewheeling nomadic existence continues with hopefully a few new sights, sounds and experiences. Simplicity and harmony itself.

Though the accommodations we stayed at were generally very good, Etienne had warned us that one place, which has since closed down, was not to the same standard as the others but that in this area there were few alternatives. On arrival this soon became apparent as the eager to please owner led us with fully laden bikes across a positively dangerous wooden bridge to a rather tired and run down room. Later they cooked us the most awful vegetarian meal of tasteless stewed vegetables, not dissimilar to the Northern English grammar school meals I endured in the 1970s. How could this be so? Surely now I was in the culinary Mecca of Thailand! Later on the bedding in the room proved inadequate to cope with the fact we were slightly at altitude and the nagging cold in the early hours made sleep fitful at best.

Having eaten little and slept poorly, Jan was immediately in trouble on the hills within about twenty minutes of setting out the next morning. I ended up taking everything in my panniers and acting as her domestique all day, constantly cycling just in front of her to protect her from the wind. The previous evening I had very sensibly shovelled down as much of the dismal meal as possible, grimacing and cursing but treating it as nothing more than fuel for the body.

Despite all this, it was a great trip and the fact it was unguided gave us much more freedom to do our own thing. Such was our state of relaxation on returning to Chiang Mai that we found the big city, with all its absurd commotion and people, quite irksome. Quite unreasonably Etienne had promptly retrieved his bikes and equipment and had left no further instructions about how to live the rest of our lives. There was only one thing for it. We returned to the lovely peaceful 'Jasmine Hills', an accommodation we discovered during the trip, for a couple of days. They serve a far superior vegetarian curry there.

CHAPTER 19
AUGUST - INDONESIAN VOLCANOES AND DRAGONS

Between Thailand and New Zealand, what better place to break your journey than Indonesia? The plan was to spend time on four islands in the far flung Indonesian Archipelago. Sumatra, Komodo, Lombok and Bali.

On Sumatra we visited Lake Toba, the largest lake in South East Asia, and Berestagi, from where we hiked up a very straightforward 2,100 metre volcano, Gunung Sibayak. Volcanoes have been in the news rather a lot in recent years, particularly Icelandic ones that have a habit of grounding aircraft all over Europe when they erupt. Indonesia is of course famous for its volcanoes, sitting as it does on the Pacific Ring of Fire, and perhaps its most famous son is Krakatau, which erupted in 1883 with such devastating consequences. Sibayak was by contrast in a gentle mood and only the sulphur laden steam from its fumaroles hinted at the power within. Though volcanoes often take life, they also support it in the form of the incredibly rich volcanic soil around their flanks. Around Sibayak it is possible to grow everything you can in the UK plus a host of tropical fruits, in fact everything except the humble apple. So if you are considering a fruit and vegetable garden and are not too bothered about making cider, Sumatra is the place to go and you won't need any fertilizer.

On the theme of natural disasters, we visited Banda Aceh, scene of the devastating tsunami in 2004. The city is completely flat and, looking at it from the sea, it is easy to see how the surge might run inland for miles, unopposed by any higher ground. Happily, the place now looks as if the disaster never happened following the international aid effort. From Banda Aceh we took a local ferry to Pulau Weh, an island on the very tip of Northern Sumatra, for centuries used by sailors from the West as a cue to steer into the narrow straits of Malacca. We did several excellent dives here before catching colds and having to rest up. The coral and fish life here is incredibly diverse.

On the old maps medieval cartographers, unsure as to what an area of the world was like but not willing to admit it, simply declared "There be dragons". Of course they were very rarely correct, except where we were headed next. Perhaps the highlight of Indonesia was a two day boat trip to Komodo National Park. This is of course home to the infamous Komodo Dragon, a powerful carnivorous lizard weighing in at up to one hundred and fifty kilos and up to three metres long. It is closely related to the tropical monitor lizard but much bigger. We opted to do the longer ranger led treks (they don't let you go off on your own) on both Rinca and Komodo islands and, as a reward, we had a ranger guide all to ourselves. We set off into the dense interior behind our guide who carried only a forked stick for protection.

On Komodo itself, half way up a mountain we rather disconcertingly came across a memorial cross to a tourist assumed taken in the 1970s by a dragon. Only his inedible glasses and camera were ever found. On Komodo thankfully they no longer feed live goats to the dragons for the benefit of tourists so we were able to observe many aspects of their natural behaviour. They are incredibly well camouflaged, lurking in the dappled shade under trees, and when a large magnificent individual pounds purposefully to within a few metres of you with its familiar confident swaggering gait it is high time to retreat behind the ranger's forked stick. Taking care not to get too close to a different dragon in the process of course. Though I suspect that the stick would not afford too much protection if the dragon were serious in its intentions. The ranger actually admitted they have been known to break sticks in the past.

Just as well that the American lady with the tiny baby had not been allowed to join the longer two or three hour trek through the bone dry forest in the intense heat. She was told in no uncertain terms by the ranger that the most she could hope to do was the short hike and then only under strict supervision. Call me a traditionalist if you will, but it's a good thing someone had a little of that most uncommon of commodities, common sense! On these hikes you really cannot afford to just switch off and need to keep your wits about you at all times. You don't need any distractions. But as long as you are sensible you'll be fine.

It's fascinating to watch the dragons as they hang around water holes, perfectly camouflaged, waiting for a prey animal to come within range before striking with their jaws. They are infinitely patient ambush predators and even bite the much larger buffaloes. Having done this, they then wait for the wound to become infected, following the stricken animal for days till it dies and they have their meal. It is very much nature in the raw. We never saw an attack and to be honest I preferred it that way.

Komodo National Park is world class below the water too. After spending four days diving here we saw many elegant Manta Rays and other large pelagics. But the currents here can be exceptionally strong with rough sea conditions and water temperatures surprisingly chilly for the tropics. You need to drift with the current, surface marker buoys inflated so the boat can track your movements. If you lose contact with the boat in the strong currents you are in big trouble. It is challenging diving, not really for novice divers.

In Indonesia our final volcano challenge was a tough three day hike and camping excursion around Gunung Rinjani, a volcanically active 4,000 metres giant in Northern Lombok. There was also an option to attempt the summit on the last day, though to do so would convert the day into a ten hour marathon. On summit day I was distinctly grumpy as we had been kept awake by a group of Asian trekkers on the campsite the night before. In the West in our National Parks there is very much an attitude that if you go into the wilderness you should seek to be calm and quiet and to blend in with your surroundings. This is not always the case in Asia where on one occasion to our horror we actually experienced karaoke!

On summit day Jan had a headache and was clearly feeling the altitude so sensibly stayed in her sleeping bag. I set out at three in the morning with our guide in order to arrive at the summit in time for day break. Fuelled initially by grumpiness, I stormed up the mountain with the young Indonesian guide, summiting first that day in two and a half hours rather than the usual three. But this success unfortunately meant we had a very cold forty minutes at the top awaiting morning's first rays of light. We quickly put on all the layers of clothing we possessed but still shivered. But when the sun did rise it was a magical place to be. In fact it is a sacred mountain for the Balinese and that morning it wasn't difficult to understand why.

Rinjani is a stunningly beautiful mountain with an enormous cobalt blue crater lake and smaller active volcano, Gunung Baru, in the middle of the vast six kilometre caldera. As we reached the rim on our descent Gunung Baru erupted, rumbling ominously and throwing up a perfect mushroom shaped plume of ash. I watched this awesome natural display from close up, perhaps no more than two kilometres, with a mixture of both fascination and horror. It was nature at its most elemental. I took my cue from the guides. As they seemed laid back so was I. But thankfully Baru had made his point about mankind's puny impotence and didn't feel he needed to go any further. To have stood there and believed that man was somehow capable of controlling nature would have been delusional to say the least. My own thoughts of ancient Pompeii and the mummified remains of its ill fated inhabitants quickly and happily receded. Tired but elated, we slowly ambled back to base camp just in time to prevent the high altitude Macaque Monkeys from devouring our well earned banana pancake breakfast. We were the kings of the mountain that day and it felt great to be alive. But, as with the old Roman Triumphs, all glory in life is fleeting, ephemeral. I really suffered towards the end of the day on the continuous descents. Was it worth it? Absolutely.

Whilst in Sumatra I had a lesson in the power of peer pressure. Because it is a Muslim area of Indonesia they do not drink. Instead many young people seem to smoke like chimneys. It seems to us that at some time in the future, maybe twenty or thirty years from now, there will be a reckoning and a major public health crisis. I often used to travel on the back seat of local buses in Sumatra where there is more leg room. Young guys would sit down, light up and often chat to me. They would often offer me a cigarette which I would politely refuse as I don't smoke. After about the sixth offer from these friendly people I came very close to accepting simply to be sociable. I have never smoked myself and both my grandfathers died prematurely because of smoking. I like to think I have an independent mind. However if all your mates are smoking you tend to do so yourself. I was so close to accepting. That's the power of peer pressure!

Whilst staying by Lake Toba we bought a couple of carvings. One is a human mask, the other a Lake Toba Dragon. They are not the sort of mass produced tat you can pick up anywhere. Though they only cost us about one hundred US dollars for the two pieces they are of excellent quality. The talented local artist was running a wood carving workshop for Western travellers at the time and we visited his gallery. The artistic quality was so uniformly good that you could have bought any item from the shop and been delighted. In Bali too around Ubud they have some wonderful works of art fashioned in wood. Unlike in the West, great art doesn't cost a fortune. I guess it's mostly down to relative labour costs.

CHAPTER 20
SEPTEMBER - RUGBY WORLD CUP IN NEW ZEALAND

As I feared, Jan had insisted from the start that we incorporate the Rugby World Cup into our proposed itinerary. I would now have to force myself, against my better judgement, to hang around stadia in New Zealand, drinking Steinlager and generally having a good time. It was a tough one but I would have to be prepared to make the ultimate sacrifice and go along with it all.

Our flight from Denpasar landed in Christchurch, South Island, New Zealand. From my window seat there were stunning views of the Southern Alps as we approached our destination. South Island was a real culture shock after the Hindu Kingdom of Bali with its temples, colourful ceremonies and gamelan orchestras. It is also much colder here as the Southern Hemisphere winter has only just very reluctantly given way to a frigid early spring. Initially on landing, as I zipped up my heavy duty fleece, I found myself questioning my sanity in coming to such a place at this time of year.

On our Air New Zealand flight from Bali to Christchurch we were greatly impressed by the pre flight safety briefing. They had a great way of making passengers sit up and pay attention. Instead of the usual briefing, delivered uninspiringly by a deeply bored member of the cabin staff, they'd made a wonderful safety video. In the video Graham Henry, New Zealand head coach, was the captain and Richie McCaw, his captain on the pitch, appeared as co pilot. Some of the members of the All Blacks with film star looks appeared in cameo roles flirting with clearly star struck Air New Zealand crew. Rugby is certainly more glamorous in New Zealand than in England. It was a nice humorous touch and served notice, just in case it had slipped anyone's mind, that we were only a few days away from the World Cup opener at Eden Park.

After picking up our hire car at Christchurch airport we headed down to Dunedin to see our old friends Marjorie and Colin. They are both retired vets and live in a lovely house with plenty of land on the outskirts of the city. On our first trip to New Zealand Colin, who had his pilot's licence, had taken us on a stunning flight in a small plane above the Otago Peninsula. Now, as welcoming as ever, they were operating a kind of open house for the duration of the World Cup whereby various waifs and strays from the UK were very kindly given accommodation. This would be our base for match days. Between matches we would leave them in peace! Colin is a keen Highlanders fan and would accompany us to a couple of the England games.

On the field the first game saw England take on the Pumas in the Scottish city of Dunedin in their brand new thirty thousand seater covered stadium. The atmosphere was building up nicely in the city centre before the game with Argentinians honking horns and waving flags in exuberant South American style. In the game itself England won an undeserved victory and, had Argentina taken their early chances, they would have lost.

The real Argentine supporters were great but less so the hordes of drunken University of Otago students who were wearing Argentina shirts but really would have supported anyone playing the English. Had a Martian First Fifteen taken to the field against England, they would have been enthusiastically wearing green! They were easy to spot as New Zealanders as they were oblivious to Argentina's quirky national anthem and, from comments like "Come on the Argies", they clearly were not students of the language of Cervantes or Gabriel Garcia Marquez. Among the general good natured banter that characterises rugby stadia the world over I suggested they may like to try instead "Vamos muchachos" to at least preserve some sort of authenticity!

The following two games were also at the splendid new Otago stadium against group minnows Georgia and Romania. This time the students were slightly better behaved in confining themselves to stamping their feet noisily and organising endless Mexican waves. Though these minor teams were certainly narrowing the gap, England as expected ran out comfortable winners. The crunch game takes place in Auckland against Scotland at the weekend.

Between games we are using our well run in but perfectly serviceable hire car to explore parts of New Zealand we have not previously visited. It is a pleasant carefree sort of life. We are staying in self catering accommodation and cooking for ourselves. Eating out is obviously much more expensive than in Bali. Accommodation is good value by UK standards despite the dire weakness of the pound. However, the changeable early season weather has not been conducive to embarking on major treks or crossing the strait to Stewart Island but we are staying very active.

Though we endured poor weather in the Catlins, that rugged coastal area between Dunedin and Invercargill, in the second week our luck changed when we headed into the highlands of Central Otago. Here we cycled and hiked large sections of the one hundred and fifty kilometre Central Otago Rail Trail. An uneconomic railway line, constructed during the Gold Rush of the nineteenth century, was recently torn up and a compacted gravel cycleway laid down. It is perfect for cycling with no incline steeper than the one in fifty a locomotive could manage yet with superb gorges and alpine scenery.

Many of the station platforms and signs are still there along with tunnels, viaducts and historic buildings such as the ladies waiting room from a hundred years ago. We had great weather and saw few other cyclists but in the summer the accommodation along the track is booked solid. It is a superb resource and the number of visitors it attracts has economically regenerated the area. So the railway has brought economic prosperity for a second time in a way the Victorian railway engineers who built it could never have envisaged. Arguably recreational cycling is more sustainable than gold mining.

We are now heading up to Christchurch to catch a flight to Auckland, following the Rugby Circus up to North Island. We will take in Mount Cook, Sir Edmund Hillary's old training ground, on the way. On my flight I shall feel a little less guilty about the environment. Under Colin's expert direction we spent a morning planting about seventy trees at his place south of Dunedin.

Everyone knows that "The Lord of the Rings" did more for New Zealand's profile than Captain Cook. In the Otago Daily Times the other day they were advertising for elves and character townspeople for "The Hobbit" shortly to be filmed on location in this area. I didn't bother applying!

CHAPTER 21
OCTOBER - THE TOURNAMENT REACHES ITS CLIMAX

Auckland with its traffic and crowds was initially a little overwhelming after the serene beauty of Mount Cook and the slower pace of life on South Island. But we had come here for a purpose, to support an England team that was playing as if it needed all the support it could get.

The matches from here on were all at Eden Park, Auckland, that great cathedral of New Zealand rugby. For in New Zealand practically everyone has an informed view on All Blacks selection and they embrace the game with almost religious zeal. In contrast to the Vatican, where it can take many centuries to be canonised for good works on earth, here it is possible to be a saint by your early thirties. Both Ritchie McCaw and Dan Carter are living proof of this phenomenon. Such devotion makes for a great tournament.

Eden Park itself, a sixty thousand seater stadium, has been specially refurbished for the tournament with temporary seating added at each end. But somewhat inexplicably, given the frequent rain, large parts of the stadium are uncovered. Here, as befits a pilgrimage, you need to be able to suffer for your team.

At the England versus Scotland match the atmosphere was electric, with the swathes of white and blue in the crowd fairly evenly matched in numbers. As usual the neutrals were supporting Scotland, on paper the underdogs. As the game progressed, with Scotland holding the lead for most of the match, the Scottish supporters (many in kilts but without their bagpipes, banned from the stadium) were highly vocal, baying for the blood of their ancient foe. However, their satisfaction proved to be short lived when a late England try sent them home early. Scotland had been unlucky and it was another unconvincing England performance. For the moment the English supporters might be singing along with gusto to the strains of "Sweet Caroline" but sooner or later their good fortune would change.

The next game saw the arrival of much more dangerous opponents in the form of France. Undoubtedly the French performance was lifted by a rousing rendition of the Marseillaise, that great call to arms forged in the heat of the Revolutionary Wars.

Not an anthem our own modest royalist hymn could hope to compete with. All the neutrals were rooting for France. Renegade Scotsmen were seeking vicarious vengeance and the Kiwis were clearly prepared to forgive the sinking of the Rainbow Warrior but could never forgive boring rugby.

Having won the anthems, the French set about winning the game and were sixteen nil up at half time. Joyous chants of "Allez les bleus" rang around Eden Park and I have to admit the French fans were great fun. Some of the wittier English fans responded with "Allez les blancs" whilst others grew steadily more morose and depressed. Some turned to alcohol in the form of Heineken, the only beer available. At £4 for a small can this was even more depressing. Despite a better second half performance from England, the French ran out worthy winners. England were out but this was not unexpected given their lacklustre performances. We'd been expecting this outcome so were not that unhappy and really enjoyed the occasion. England's style of play had won them few friends.

Overall New Zealand proved themselves head and shoulders above the rest of the world and rightly recorded their first World Champions title since 1987 despite a brilliant French performance in the final. That night at Eden Park the feeling of tension amongst the Kiwis was palpable. In the press there had been much national soul searching beforehand. Were the Kiwis poor losers? Was their sense of national identity too narrowly defined? How would their national psyche cope with another four years of not being World Champions? In the end it was all idle speculation as the All Blacks recorded a narrow victory against the valiant French, amidst scenes of wild celebration at Eden Park.

With all the excitement now over, people can start considering who to vote for in the now imminent General Election. During all the euphoria of the rugby tournament the politicians had very sensibly not bored the electorate with any of the mundane election issues. Democracy had been put on hold through lack of interest! Nobody was complaining.

Between games we toured around North Island, though the often rainy conditions meant we had to scale back our ambitions. It rains a lot in New Zealand. Despite this we visited the northern Kauri forests, the Coromandel Peninsula and Cape Reinga at the very top of North Island.

One highlight was finally seeing the elusive Kiwi bird, an endangered flightless bird and symbol of the nation. In the wild they are difficult to see, being both now few in numbers and nocturnal by nature. I have to confess that we cheated and went to the Kiwi House at Auckland Zoo. In this simulated nocturnal environment the Kiwi bird is deceived into thinking it is night time so that people can see it foraging for food during the day. They are actually distant smaller relatives of the ostrich and are endangered due to the predation of their chicks by non native mammals introduced by the usual suspect, man. Great effort and expense is made to ensure their precarious foothold does not deteriorate further. Everyone who visits New Zealand should try to see a Kiwi bird.

Before returning home we still have Tonga, Fiji, Tahiti and Easter Island to look forward to. It's tough but someone has to do it.

CHAPTER 22
NOVEMBER - SAILING IN TONGA

The highlight of our time in Polynesia was undoubtedly our week of sailing in the Kingdom of Tonga's Vavau Group of islands.

We had arrived in Tonga immediately after the World Cup hoping to swim with Humpback Whales but, on arrival, learnt that most of them had very unreasonably just commenced their summer migration to Antarctica. We'd missed them by a matter of days. Though we never saw any of those that did remain we did hear distant whale song underwater whilst diving. It is an amazingly haunting and mournful song. Though the whale was distant (the song will carry for many kilometres underwater) its song was quite distinct if you temporarily stopped breathing into your regulator.

However, every cloud has a silver lining. If we were

out of season for the whales it was precisely the right time to go sailing. During the whale watching season it can apparently get very busy with many boats competing for anchorages. But at the start of November most boats, like the whales, head south to New Zealand ahead of the cyclone season in December. As long as the cyclones didn't arrive early all would be well.

With our certificates from Thailand we had decided to do "Bareboat charter" whereby you simply hire or charter a yacht without a skipper, relying essentially on your own skill, experience and decision making. During an hour long briefing with the charter company we were handed a chart that said "Not to be used for navigational purposes". Following a further boat briefing on our Jeanneau thirty three footer we were invited to get on with it. They suggested the first night's anchorage and beyond that all we had to do was radio in our chosen anchorage at four in the afternoon every day. All anchorages are numbered and designated as suitable for day or night use. The night use anchorages are better and more protected. We should also listen to the weather forecast every morning on the VHF at eight thirty. This seemed a very sensible thing to do.

Contrary to popular myth, sailing is not really very glamorous. Conditions are inevitably fairly cramped compared to dry land and, at least until you get used to it, you are forever banging your head on low doorways and stubbing your toes. You find yourself cursing and swearing when the second anchor, put down for extra holding, becomes hopelessly caught up with the main anchor. Even when disentangled it still has to be freed from the sea bed by a heroic lung bursting free dive without fins to seven metres. This was the last time we used the second anchor! Furthermore, it often seems pretty clear that boat designers and engineers all work in an office as far away from the sea as possible.

But if it isn't glamorous it does give you some wonderful freedom to explore seascapes of incredible natural beauty. Tonga with its protected waters is considered to be amongst the best sailing areas in the world. It is a classic Polynesian picture postcard paradise. Here rocky islands covered in lush tropical vegetation and palm trees cascade to narrow sandy beaches that practically disappear at high water.

However, it is also a potentially dangerous place with many treacherous shoals and reefs. They are at least marked on the chart and in sunny conditions you can pick out the tell tale turquoise and browns from the dark blue of the deeper water. Often you can pick out shallow water from where the waves are breaking. This sort of visual recognition is not so easy in rainy or overcast conditions.

Our favourite anchorage was number sixteen. Apart

from its beauty, it has a patch of sand where the anchor can securely hold about seventy meters off the shore so you don't need to approach the coral heads near the beach too closely. From here you can go ashore in the dinghy. It is also very well protected from the prevailing South East trade winds, ensuring a comfortable night's sleep.

At exactly six forty five each evening the cicadas in the nearby trees start their deafening chorus, signalling the sun is over the yard arm and it's time to pour a couple of glasses of Tongan coconut rum as the boat swings lazily at anchor and large flying foxes are taking to the air. In uncertain light winds the boat will often do a complete circle as the bow fretfully seeks out the wind, presenting an ever changing vista as you sit on deck and admire the perfection of this place.

Then something to eat whilst watching the sky change colour as the sun dips down. You are completely alone. However, the sea will never let you relax totally as any sign of a dragging anchor quickly snaps you out of such reveries. This beach also has a black dog that you can take for walks at low tide. He is such a good swimmer he sometimes follows your tender as you row back to the yacht, despite all attempts to turn him back for his own safety. He swims around your yacht seventy metres off the shore in ten metres of water before heading back to the safety of his beach.

The other great highlight of Polynesia was diving with Bull Sharks in Fiji's Beqa Lagoon. Bull Sharks have a reputation for ferocity and aggression and have been known to kill people. So the organised shark feeding dive was a chance for us to make up our own minds as to whether this reputation was justified.

There were many nervous looks exchanged between the divers on the rough boat ride out to the lagoon, with the sense of humour being of a distinctly gallows nature. There were the inevitable references to wills and to seeking absolution from priests. Everyone was laughing just a little too loudly. This is the sort of enterprise that could never happen in the UK, where a health and safety culture advises strongly against such perilous activities as getting out of bed in the morning.

However, this Fijian operation managed the risks brilliantly. There was a thorough briefing about exactly what to expect and what not to do (like waving your arms around during feeding), at the end of which divers were given the opportunity not to proceed if they were unhappy. The divemaster feeding the sharks wore an extended chain mail glove for protection. Other staff members would take up positions behind the divers to protect them with steel poles if necessary. Five metres from the surface there would be a spare tank and regulator for a decompression stop in case anyone panicked and ran out of air. It was all very professional. They even warned us about the Chinese divers on the other boat. They were apparently much more dangerous than the Bull Sharks themselves as, due to poor technique, they were quite likely to accidentally knock your mask off with a flailing fin.

We entered the water and once everyone was happy we descended rapidly to about thirty metres. The divers lay on a patch of sand on their bellies with gloved hands close to our bodies. A few metres further down the reef the divemaster started to feed the soon swirling mass of tropical fish. Before long the first Bull Shark arrived. Though massive it was a little cautious of the divers. It cruised around and eventually took a tuna head from the divemaster with the gentleness of a playful puppy. Nothing like "Jaws" at all. Another half a dozen Bull Sharks soon came in and almost politely took food. At one point one approached a diver a little too closely and as a precaution was warded off with a rod. After ten minutes at thirty metres we retreated up the reef to decompress. We decompressed whilst watching a second feeding session at about ten metres but these Bull Sharks like deep water and did not follow us up the reef. Here we only saw the much smaller Grey Reef Sharks, Whitetips, Blacktips and Silvertips.

The marine biologist on the boat has identified and named more than one hundred and twenty different

Bull Sharks. These enormous sharks have innocuous and genteel sounding names like Valerie, Grandma, Blunt and Chunky. The females are larger than the males and Grandma is a massive three and a half metres. She is so stocky that I estimate she weighs about ten times what a Grey Reef Shark would. Though powerful and barrel chested she still retains incredible beauty and grace in the water like all sharks. They are so elegant and well adapted to their environment.

These sessions are not without controversy in that some argue that sharks may come to associate people with food, which may make them more likely to attack. But people are a much greater risk to sharks than vice versa. We kill millions of sharks each year compared to maybe a dozen fatal shark attacks. So it is fairly obvious who the mindless killing machines are. Clearly anything that helps to improve their image is a good thing and I guarantee that if you don't love sharks before this dive you certainly will afterwards.

The point about sharks is that as the top predators they maintain the integrity of the marine ecosystem and keep the oceans healthy. Given that mankind needs the sea as a source of fish protein, to persecute sharks on the present scale is an act of almost unprecedented stupidity and short sightedness.

CHAPTER 23
NOVEMBER - POLYNESIAN PARADISE

Is there anywhere in the world more exotic and romantic than Tahiti? This is the place that HMS Bounty sailed to in 1789 to collect and transport breadfruit plants to the West Indies. Fletcher Christian and his mates decided they preferred the local women and laid back way of life in these parts to the severe brand of naval discipline meted out on board ship by Captain Bligh. Having set Bligh adrift they ended up scuttling the Bounty at Pitcairn Island, well to the east where they assumed the British Navy would never find them. Their descendants still live there today. Tahiti is also the place where Paul Gauguin came to live, to contemplate life and to paint his iconic post impressionist canvasses that will be forever associated with French Polynesia.

Though I've never had a boss quite as bad as Captain

Bligh (I recall one, a six foot eight Old Harrovian, who could perhaps have given him a run for his money) what better place to take a hard earned break from work? We'd actually come here twenty years before in what now seemed like a previous life. As we were presently heading east across the Pacific anyway, we decided to schedule a stop off for old time's sake and to break down the vastness of the Pacific into manageable segments. We were keen to see if anything much had changed in this Polynesian paradise. How was Elysium these days?

As our taxi took us from Papeete airport to our hotel I looked out at the riot of tropical vegetation, thought again of Gauguin's paintings and tried to remember what we'd done on our previous visit.

I remember us pitching up late at a campsite outside of Papeete on our first night, so late it was going dark. We struggled to pitch our North Face tent in the dark, only saved by the fact we'd done it so many times in daylight. During the night we heard a scream. I peered out of the tent and discovered that a very large land crab had got into a neighbouring tent, leaving the occupant in a state of distress. In reality I expect the poor thing was more terrified than her. With the land crab suitably sent on its way we all went back to sleep.

I remembered Monsieur Tamatona, a likeable and eccentric French chef with a local wife. We spent a week camping on his property and enjoying his fine cooking on Rangiroa. One night, very uncharacteristically, they'd had a shouting match just outside our tent. I wondered if he was still around.

Were there still lots of Grey Reef Sharks around Rangiroa Atoll? I recalled clearly our first dive as, having descended to around twenty five metres, we shot Tiputa pass at about ten knots. The French dive guide had sensibly warned us to expect many sharks swimming very closely in between the divers. What he could not have predicted was Jan's practical joke as she mischievously grabbed the back of my leg, and the look on my face as I lunged round to face my assailant! It was all coming back.

Then there was the eighteen hour boat trip on a supply ship from Papeete to Bora Bora. We'd slept on deck staring up at the Southern Cross, snuggled down in our sleeping bags and using our rucksacks as pillows. The fact it started to rain didn't seem to matter. We loved every minute of the trip. In those days we had a tight budget and were proper backpackers! We'd put up with any hardship just to experience new things. These days I'm afraid we need a bit more comfort.

Once settled in our comfortable hotel we soon discovered that nothing much had changed really. The sea was still the same impossibly vibrant shade of cobalt blue that seems to distinguish the Pacific from other oceans around the world. French Polynesia is still just as expensive. Whilst other areas, such as Hawaii, had grown their tourist numbers in the time since our last visit the numbers visiting Tahiti remained flat. It's expensive to get to because of its location and imported goods from France are not cheap because of the distances. The low number of tourists does make for a very select experience if you can afford it, though it's sad that more people cannot enjoy its unique beauty. On our previous visit the French were pretty much hated all over the Pacific. One positive change was that at least now they had finally stopped exploding nuclear bombs on Moruroa Atoll, once a natural paradise but sadly now a radioactive man made hell. It certainly took them long enough. The people of the area are still suffering radiation linked health issues and continue to pay a heavy price for France's post war self delusional great power status. These proud but poor citizens of the Republic have received precious little compensation for the hubris of De Galle and Chirac. Let alone an apology. Moruroa is now surely at least the equal of Vichy in terms of shame for this great nation.

In the same Tuamotu Archipelago but very distant from Moruroa are three atolls, Tikehau, Rangiroa and Fakarava. On this trip we had decided to do some diving on each atoll. In contrast to Tahiti these atolls are rocky, barren places with poor beaches and sparse vegetation. You would have to be crazy to come here for a standard beach holiday. But as a diver you would be crazy not to visit. Fakarava in particular has excellent coral, enormous shoals of fish and hundreds of reef sharks. It is full of staggeringly good dive sites. On our return to Rangiroa we saw our first Hammerhead Shark and we were visited by a large solitary dolphin. He was in playful mood and stayed with us for several minutes, generally showing off his all round superiority in the water. In Rangiroa the coral is actually very poor but you have the justified impression that virtually any large pelagic could turn up on any dive at any time. You have to be careful. If you spot a Manta Ray at forty metres you have to be mindful to monitor your depth gauge and air as you will need to spend plenty of time decompressing before going to the surface. With so much wonder going on around you it would be easy to forget this. Ever conscious of the risk of getting the bends, we dive with two dive computers and obey the one that gives us the slowest ascent rate. There may possibly be better places to dive than French Polynesia but not in this world.

We are now fully desaturated of excess nitrogen in our bodies. We are therefore safe to fly tomorrow from Fakarava back to Papeete and then on to Easter Island, sadly the final destination on our marathon trip.

CHAPTER 24
DECEMBER - EASTER ISLAND'S MOAI MYSTERY

It is a tiny speck of land dwarfed by the enormity of the Pacific, a full three thousand miles off the coast of South America at the southeasternmost point of the Polynesian Triangle. It's a place with a dark history that had fascinated me for as long as I can remember. Of all the places I'd dreamt of when we planned our trip, this was the place I really wanted to visit more than any other. It's hard to really say why. Was it the remoteness of the location? If it was a sense of history it wasn't conventional or written history, often the only history valued by our Western civilisation, as this does not exist here. Both those things had brought us here but, more than anything else, it was its profound sense of mystery.

The mystery is this. When the first Europeans arrived on the island on Easter Sunday 1722 they found enormous monolithic human figures, known as moai, all over the island. Most of them had been toppled and were laying horizontally in various states of decay on their back, face or side. Some showed evidence of having been burned. There were so many questions. Who had sculpted and transported the stone heads and why? Where did these people come from? How had they managed to move such heavy pieces of stone from the quarries to their pedestals many miles away? Why were there so few trees on the island? Having gone to such trouble why on earth did they eventually seek to destroy their precious moai? The questions go on and on.

Thor Heyerdahl called Easter Island the most remote inhabited place on earth. Nowadays it is not quite as remote as when Thor visited. The airport runway is big enough to take 747s courtesy of the US Space Program. A couple of times a week LAN Chile use it as a stopover between French Polynesia and Santiago. This is a journey that would normally take about twelve hours across the vastness of the Pacific but you can very conveniently split the long journey in two by staying on Easter Island for a few days. Perfect.

Where to start? There's only one place to start here, of course, once the jet lag has gone. With the archaeology. Tours are available but we spent several hours in the excellent Rapa Nui Museum bringing ourselves up to date with the island's archaeology and the various theories as to what might have happened here.

Next we needed to get out to the sites. We managed to hire some half decent bikes and spent the next four days cycling around the different archaeological sites. Given its small size you can easily cycle around the island in a day and there is not much traffic around. It's perfect for cycling. The place is remote and incredibly atmospheric. The eyes of the all knowing moai seem to track your every movement as many of the fallen statues have now been resurrected.

At Ahu Tongariki you cycle the deserted southern road, trying to avoid the free grazing sleepy horses, and then suddenly come upon an amazing group of about fifteen moai, all staring impassively inland with the limitless cobalt blue of the Pacific stretching away in the background. One of them weighs nearly ninety tons. It's an impressive place, on a par with Stonehenge. At Ahu Anakena there is a smaller group of moai, again facing inland, but this time with palm trees nearby and a fabulous sandy beach and turquoise shallows. You can swim here and the original Polynesian colonisers are said to have landed on this beach. In fact, if you look at the jagged coastline it's about the only place they could have come ashore in their canoes. It is these Polynesian ancestors and their descendants that the great stone statues were built to honour. There are moai scattered all over the island in various states of disrepair, some laying on their side broken or incomplete and others standing.

There is also a moai "Factory" or quarry where abandoned moai in various stages of construction can be seen. What dark cataclysmic event stopped them being finished you ask yourself? At Orongo Ceremonial Village there is the crater of a long extinct volcano and a view point overlooking Bird Island. Hundreds of years ago there was an annual race to swim out to Bird Island and bring back the first Sooty Tern egg of the new season. The event is believed to have been part of a culturally important Birdman cult. This wonderfully atmospheric place is constantly channelling your thoughts back into the past. You almost want to scream at the inscrutable moai "What happened here, tell me?" But the moai remain silent and keep their counsel.

This is the enigma within the riddle that is Easter Island. The oral history passed down through the generations was brutally disjointed in the nineteenth century by slave traders and European diseases. The population was virtually wiped out and with it the knowledge of what really happened. Sadly, we are now reduced to inspired guesswork.

There is one interesting theory worth mentioning. Easter Island was once full of forests but now there is very little tree cover. The moving and erecting of such enormous stone statues would have required the felling of huge numbers of trees. Did an increasing population require the manufacture of more and more moai to honour their increasing number of ancestors? Did they simply run out of resource when all the trees were gone, with not enough wood even to construct the fishing boats to go fishing? Did wars then break out between tribes over access to these scarce and precious resources? Did rival factions topple and burn each others moai in the civil war or did they collectively reject the entire cult of ancestor worship that had brought about such disaster? In such a remote place there would have been nowhere to go in order to escape the violence, particularly if they lacked the material to build boats. Even with boats they would have been three thousand miles from South America or other parts of Polynesia.

If the above theory is correct this could prove to be a cautionary tale for modern man about not expanding population, religion and culture beyond what is sustainable and the wise use of limited natural resources. We perhaps need to look more closely at what happened here if future generations are to have a viable future on our small fragile planet. If we ignore history we may be condemned to repeat it. Maybe I'll send a copy of this update to the Vatican for starters. Their stance on contraception is looking increasingly irresponsible as we enter the third millennium.

On a lighter note, we have managed to befriend the guest house owner's large Alsatian dog, Michigan. He has a lovely temperament and we've been taking him on walks around the island. He seems to have a distinct territory in which he is the alpha male. At the end of this invisible territorial boundary he simply stops and refuses to go any further. He's a very useful friend to have at night. Later on, we like to sleep with the door open due to the heat. If you invite Michigan to lie just inside the doorway you can have a cool environment and sleep well, safe in the knowledge you are fully protected. It's going to be a tight fit getting him into our hand luggage!

Sadly, we fly to Santiago tomorrow and, after a brief stopover, back to London. See you soon.

CHAPTER 25
EPILOGUE - RETURNING HOME

Air traffic congestion in the south east of England found us sitting expectantly in a stack above Heathrow, flying in a holding pattern above the gently rolling land of the south. We'd long since lost the will to live. It would be another twenty minutes before air traffic control would allow us to land. Tired and a little dehydrated from the long flight back from Santiago, I struggled to coherently order my thoughts.

The party was over. Would there be a hangover? The truth is I'd never really wanted the experience to end. I'd never felt more alive. Searching desperately for the positives, it would be good to see family and friends. Apart from that I hadn't really missed the UK much, other than the odd nostalgic reminiscence of wandering into a country pub and ordering a pint of real ale.

We'd had an amazing adventure. By way of contrast all our friends would be doing pretty much the same routine jobs and talking about the same old things as when we'd left. Their jobs, the kids, the latest election or referendum, the travails of their favourite football team and, of course, the national obsession, the weather. Our travels would be just another topic of conversation to be briefly commented on before moving onto the next subject. Just like someone else's annual vacation. Some may not even know we'd been away. Faced with such indifference how would we feel?

Also how would we adjust to a more normal type of existence on our return? When you travel of course every day is different and stimulating. Would we find the routine of everyday life irksome and oppressive?

Speaking of routine, what would we do about the thorny issue of work? We'd decided we didn't want permanent jobs. We were getting too old for putting in all the unpaid hours and playing the silly office politics. All that tedious baggage that comes with a career these days. Besides, I would find it uncomfortable to declare at an interview that, having been travelling for a year, travel was now fully out of my system. If anything the exact opposite was true. The truth was we were even more addicted to this drug than a year earlier. I suppose as addictions go it's not a bad one to have, rather like becoming addicted to endorphins when you exercise. I'd prefer to call it a passion.

How much money did we really need to survive given the mortgage was long since paid off and we have no kids? The modern world operates a curious sort of economic system. There are some very clever marketing people around whose job is to persuade you that you really need all sorts of ridiculous goods and services which you plainly don't. Credit is too freely available from banks and credit card companies. So you buy all these items you don't really need on credit. That means you have to work harder to repay interest and capital. This leads to stress. To combat the stress you find you need to buy more things. You deserve it. You have to work even harder then. The cycle goes on and on. The great hamster wheel of materialistic capitalism. It doesn't really make you happy. If only people would save up first and then spend their hard earned money on life enhancing experiences I can't help thinking they'd all be much happier. If only people were just a little less like sheep.

If we worked at all we would do so on our own terms. This would mean contract work. No lying at interview. We would simply undertake to do the job for the duration of the contract to the best of our abilities. We would leave it to the more politically astute to play the politics. Whilst they are scheming their way to corporate glory we will be planning our next trip, indulging our great passion.

But, having saved our money, where would we travel to next? How could we possibly match what we had just done? We wouldn't need to. If we lived to be a hundred there would always be a plethora of fascinating new places to visit. There would also be places so interesting that we would simply have to return. There would always be a compelling reason to bid a temporary farewell to the white cliffs of Dover. I think we both accept with resignation that the UK will always be our base from which to explore. We know the system here and its post colonial eccentricities all too well. And, having travelled, we will look at our own country in a different light and from a new perspective, rather as a foreigner might. This has to be a good thing.

"Cabin crew, prepare for landing please".

I smile wistfully and think of the nightmare that had been the catalyst for the trip. Scary stuff. But all was now well. In fact, I'd recently received an email from a very excited Graham saying how good the Pamplona experience had been. He has finally run with his bulls. He's talking about taking a motor bike up onto the Bolivian Altiplano next.

It was great that we'd given ourselves the opportunity to run with our own bulls before it was too late. I'm fine now with whatever happens in life. When the Reaper finally comes knocking on my door I can look him in the eye now, and maybe even manage a faint smile. In any event, we'll never regret what we've done. It's been a wonderful trip and I hope we've travelled in the right way. Maybe one day I'll write a book about it. And paint in oils some of the scenes from our photo album.

By now it's the start of winter. Our jackets have been strategically packed at the top of our rucksacks for easy access. It's only five degrees outside. Nothing much will be growing in our garden, though uniquely among our shrubs the Winter Jasmine should be in full bloom, its yellow flowers defiantly illuminating the seasonal gloom.

The pilot hits the runway hard, breaking noisily before commencing the long taxi to Terminal Five. It's a textbook landing, though not as exciting as our landing at Jomsom. I turn to Jan. We both smile. A special moment frozen in the amber of time. Like the Winter Jasmine we'd be just fine. The future looks bright.

David Kitching

ABOUT THE AUTHOR

David Kitching was born in Preston, Lancashire and brought up in Blackpool. He was educated at King Edward VII school, Lytham and read law at Cambridge University.

He is now a retired accountant and lives with his wife in a quiet village in Surrey. When not in the UK they travel extensively.

'Running With the Bulls' is David's first novel.

Printed in Great Britain
by Amazon